T0128392

WHY DIFFERENT?

A Culture of Two Subjects

SEMIOTEXT(E) FOREIGN AGENTS SERIES
JIM FLEMING & SYLVÈRE LOTRINGER, EDITORS

WHY DIFFERENT?

A Culture of Two Subjects

Interviews with Luce Irigaray

Edited by Luce Irigaray and Sylvère Lotringer

Translated by Camille Collins

Semiotext(e)

Special thanks to Tracy Adam, Heidi Bostic,
Peter Carravetta, Ben Meyers, and Stephen Pluhacek.

Semiotext(e)   Autonomedia Distribution

www.semiotexte.org   www.autonomedia.org

ISBN 978-1-570-27099-4 (pb.:alk.paper)

CONTENTS

INTRODUCTION

The questions I am asked about my books can vary according to the country of origin, the culture, the background and the sex of whomever is asking. It is therefore interesting to gather together questions of journalists, women and men, from various countries and newspapers, with those of students and socio-political partners. Although not an exhaustive sample of the existing differences, this collection allows for some of them to be revealed. Questions raised from France, Italy, and the United States, just to mention the cultures represented in this volume, are not expressed in the same way. Women's questions often differ from men's. I can hardly imagine a journalist who would ask: "How do you come up with the titles of your books?" without involving questions related to the emancipation or liberation of the female gender.

For years, I have often been criticized for saying something that may be valid for my culture but not for another, the Anglo-Saxon culture, for instance. In their diversity, these interviews all run along the same lines. Furthermore, world-wide gatherings of women indicate a convergence in the requests addressed to political powers, as well as in the specific goals, and this even from Far-Eastern or African women. Levels of emancipation obviously vary, but women's liberation is truly a universal problem, and differences between cultures often depend on a certain degree of subjection and oppression of the feminine sex or gender by patriarchy, or a masculine identity conceived as authoritarian and imperialistic.

I could have added other interviews. I will do so in coming volumes, and opposition to fundamental questions concerning the feminine identity, its relations of alliance and kinship with the masculine subject and its social and cultural roles will prove to be a resistance, rather than the sign of a truly different tradition.

Diachronic evolution itself raises interesting problems. In more ancient civilizations, women assumed a more valorous status than they do today. We should not, however, confuse the woman with the mother, especially man's mother. It is also important to look at things in terms of a relationship between genders rather than a mere analysis of the mechanisms of domination by one sex over the other involving historical reversals, which would prevent the two genders from building a horizontal relationship between them, instead of a hierarchical one.

It would also be interesting to compare the questions, as a part of the spoken language, which emphasize variable elements of discourse, as well as the dialogical relationship between people.

A collection of interviews is also of interest because it shows aspects of thought that are implicit in written texts. Being more synthetic, written texts elude presuppositions, cross-references and contextualization that can be revealed through questions asked in an interview. The pedagogical function of such a book is thus neither negligible nor even secondary. It is complementary to books that are more rigorously theoretical, more concise, implying the knowledge of an itinerary, work, methods, culture.

An interview allows a person to say something else, to say something in a different way. It gives a different access to the progression of thought. The interaction between speaker and listener also requires movements forward and backward which give another density or fluidity to what is being said. The same meaning is expressed but sometimes it seems so different that some people hardly recognize it, and will understand what remained obscure or opaque when expressed in other words, in another kind of reasoning, in a different style.

Weaving ties with people asking questions involves weaving ties with an audience that goes much beyond them. Interviewers gather together questions heard here and there, queries present in collective opinion. They are rarely exclusively personal questions. And, if they were, they would encompass those that other readers in other places and in other circles, wonder about themselves. Very few people realize that their questions or criticisms are those of many other people. There is nothing surprising about that: these questions and criticisms are conceived in an historical context which elicits their formulation, as a means of explaining or resisting. Answers given to journalists are therefore addressed to readers of both sexes, audiences of both sexes, students and researchers. They are conceived and expressed with this intention in mind, and I have put them together in one volume for that purpose. I know that they will dispel perplexities that otherwise would have been brought to my attention in letters, in seminars, in conversations, by somebody or other, here or there. Reading these interviews will provide handy explanations and a better understanding of my work, and also lead to other questions that are more demanding, more personal.

It may also be helpful to comment on one's own intellectual progression and research. Who, better than the author, can explain the choice of a word, the sequence of a discourse, the ambiguity and becoming of a meaning? I shudder at the thought of certain mistakes made in the interpretation of a sentence, a paragraph, a book. It seems to me

9

that these mistakes make understanding the work impossible, they delay its reception. In this respect, how can I not evoke the misunderstanding, provoked by *Speculum's* subtitle, which I became aware of later on, and to which I devote part of the chapter "The other: woman" in *I Love to You*? Realizing this did not diminish my gratitude towards those who devote time to translating and commenting on my books. But the novelty, precision and concision of those texts justify my decision to explain them myself at times. It also gives me an opportunity to specify the cultural genealogy in which I place myself. While I am credited with some theoretical sources which are actually quite foreign to my work, other readings are not adequately acknowledged in the interpretation of my work. Some people invent my spiritual fathers and mothers. I will keep their names unduly silent – while others are not acknowledged even when I quote them, dedicate a chapter to them, or even an entire volume. This stems from, among other things, the fact that the philosophical dimension of my writings is not sufficiently taken into account (as Margaret Whitford judiciously signaled at the beginning of her book, *Luce Irigaray: Philosophy in the Feminine*[1]), nor is the innovative nature of my thinking widely accepted.

Another reason for misinterpretation comes from giving insufficient attention to the fact that "women's liberation" requires an exacting cultural effort, and not just strategies for social emancipation. Deconstructing the patriarchal tradition is certainly indispensable, but is hardly enough. It is necessary to define new values directly or indirectly suitable to feminine subjectivity and to feminine identity. This is not an easy task. We need to go back a few steps in order to analyze the grip on the feminine subject by one or many tradition(s) created by a sole subject, *de facto* masculine, and interpret the reasons for women's absence in the definition of dominant cultural values. Why didn't they actively participate in elaborating these values? Why did they let their own values be covered up by masculine creations? And how can we ally this going back, in order to interpret and critique History, with the invention of new meanings, new codes that are not just an attempt to reverse values, but allow for both the coexistence and the fruitful encounter of two different identities? How can we get out of these false dilemmas: difference equals hierarchy, deconstruction excludes the definition of values that escape the same critiques as the ones deconstructed, etc. Sometimes it seems that opening a new horizon of thought has been made unthinkable by the influx of the new which submerges us on other levels. The horizon has to change before a culture that cares about existence, presence, intervention in the world and the relationship between two different subjects comes about. It won't just happen through social critiques and street riots. We need to go above and beyond: understanding that the human subject, woman or man, is not a mere social effect, whatever its impact and historical importance. And, whosoever renounces the specificity of both the feminine subjectivity and identity, reducing them to simple social determinations, sacrifices even more women to patriarchy. It is important to secure time to think this over, with other methods than those already used by the masculine subject. In this respect, and many others, I find it useful to dialogue in person with both male and female interviewers and to have the opportunity to explain the complexity of the course I take, the subtlety of its stakes, the novelty and difficulty of the questions that are raised, including questions of method. A collection of interviews has its place next to volumes which are less explicit on this subject.

This book was put together by weaving chronological order and thematic order. A thematic order often corresponds to the objective of a text or book that has recently been published in France or Italy. The choice of interviews is obviously partial: they deal more with the latest works rather than with prior works, the '80s and '90s rather than the '70s. One interview, published in 1979, follows the publication of *And One Doesn't Move Without the Other,* a book that addresses certain difficulties in the relationship between daughter and mother; the need to rethink these relationships is also approached in a later interview (1993) for the journal of a Catholic women's movement, and not for a daily paper of the French left. Two interviews deal with the sexuation of language, following the publication in French (1985) of *Speaking is Never Neutral* and *Sexes and Genders Through Languages,* first published in French in 1990. Two interviews that were done in 1990 deal with the issue of the symbolic (following the double issue of *Il divino concepito da noi* that I put together for the Italian journal *Inchiesta*) and also with the respective importance of both History and philosophy for the liberation of the feminine subject. A magazine for the general public, *Familles rurales,* interviewed me about *Thinking the Difference.* Three interviews deal with *I Love to You* (published in French in 1992 and in Italian in 1993), and three deal with *To Be Two* (published in Italian in 1994 and in French in 1997) with some questions concerning *I Love to You.* Four interviews evoke the question of breath in *The Breath of the Women* (1996 in France and 1997 in Italy), in the Italian version of *The Forgetting of Air* (1996), and in *Tra Oriente e Occidente* (*Between East and West*) (first Italian edition in 1997). A long interview conducted by Stephen Pluhacek and Heidi Bostic, from Purdue University, led me to refer to most of the books published during this period (1996), as the bibliography that follows the interview shows.

INTRODUCTION

I would like to thank all the people who dedicated time, energy and intelligence in formulating and asking me questions. I hope that they will be happy to find these questions in this book, which will give a greater audience and a longer duration to both their work and our exchanges.

Luce Irigaray
Paris, January 25, 1998

RELATIONSHIPS BETWEEN DAUGHTER(S) AND MOTHER(S)

Concerning *And One Doesn't Stir Without the Other* (*Et l'une ne bouge pas sans l'autre,* 1979) and some chapters from *Sexes and Genealogies* (*Sexes et Parentés,* 1987).

From "Mothers and Daughters as Seen by Luce Irigaray" (*Libération,* May 21, 1979) and "If Only Daughter and Mother Spoke to One Another" (*Horizon femme,* November–December, 1993).

1

MOTHERS AND DAUGHTERS

MARTINE STORTI / MARIE-ODILE DELACOUR: How can the mother-daughter couple stop being dark, conflictual, suffocating? How can we make a genealogy of women? How can we get out of the feminism "crisis"? In a book that just came out, *And One Doesn't Stir Without the Other*, you presents a new view on the mother/daughter couple. This book about the Italian film *Maternale* depicts both mother and daughter as each other's prisoner, and tries to establish a subject-to-subject relationship between daughter and mother. "I would love it if we were both here, for the one not to disappear in the other. So that we might be able to taste each other, touch each other, feel each other, listen to each other, see ourselves together."

"Bring out the woman in our mothers," you add. In order to shed light on that which, even among women's movements, has remained in the shadows. This would perhaps indicate a way out of what is known today as the "crisis," or the impasse of feminism. This impasse also refers to an objective situation where women will once more be the casualty of economic recession, with the (beatific) return home, the wait for the third child and the reconsideration of their right to make decisions about their own body. Strange repetition, as if we were condemned to fight the same battles over and over again.

Your book starts out with an ambiguous sentence: "With your milk, mother, it is ice I drank." What does that mean?

LUCE IRIGARAY: I see the mother-daughter relationship as the dark continent of dark continents. The darkest point of our social order. I don't know one woman who isn't suffering in her relationship with her mother. And, most often, this suffering is expressed through tears and screams. It translates into a silence between mother and daughter, as well as an inability to identify with each other. The daughter tries her best to find an image in her mother that's both similar and different, but she finds herself in front of an empty mirror. This is what "With your milk, mother, I drank ice" means.

M. STORTI / O. DELACOUR: The mother is simultaneously absent and too present. There's something like a blackmail, even a power relationship between a mother and her child: "I give you food, hence I can have a right over your life"...

L. IRIGARAY: The majority of us suffered from overprotective mothers. This is what paralyzed them, as their mothers were... Because this investment corresponded to a prescribed and guilty mothering and not to a relationship of desire and love between two people. Depersonalized mothering, an abstract function, where power therefore is limitless. What's missing here is the singular image of one woman who is also a mother. Hence the menacing fantasies attached to the maternal function. The fear of falling into a chasm, plunging into darkness, entering a magical universe. This certainly evokes an "in utero" regression, and especially the fact that we're touching there on a part of the social that's submerged, lacking language and symbolization. The woman-mother finds herself assimilated to a dark continent where reproduction and the afterlife occur. Yet again, a role deprived of any distinctive identity.

M. STORTI / O. DELACOUR: In this society, doesn't a woman stop being a woman the moment she becomes a mother? How could it be otherwise? When she refuses the maternal model, she finds herself faced with nothing...

L. IRIGARAY: At the bottom of it all, we're lacking a genealogy of women. What we know is the nuclear family which operates on the triangle father-mother-son. What's at stake is the production, reproduction and transmission of possessions. The daughter, in this situation, seems to be the loose coin, the currency of exchange. She doesn't pass on the father's name, the cultural heritage, or the wealth (except in some cases). So, she's going to be torn from her family, from her mother, in order to ensure the genealogy of her husband-father. By re-establishing a genealogy of women, we're questioning the patriarchal order. We, daughters, should challenge our mothers to be women. If we don't pay more attention to liberating the mother-daughter relationship, we risk renewing blind spots of tradition while contesting our traditional enslavement to maternity. This could explain some hang-ups, paralyses, rivalries between us, which play in the hand of power. Certainly, we've talked about our mothers among ourselves. To have a dialogue with them is another story... yet another place where we have to connect the private and the political. But this is what our struggles are about. And, for us, it's not about letting ourselves be locked into the alternative: either militant or mother, women's liberation or regressing into traditional mothering.

M. STORTI / O. DELACOUR: In women's movements, a questioning about the mother has developed whereas the "movement" itself may have acted as a replacement mother.

L. IRIGARAY: We've always known this substitutive function. For a daughter, the only way to relate to her mother would be to have children, to come to the same place, to take her place. Freud says that the little girl turns away from her mother, "hates" her. How could it be any other way in a genealogy that's exclusively patriarchal? This means that the relationship of the daughter to the mother "aborts," that the daughter "aborts" in her sexual identity. She's got nothing left but a blind mimicry and not a relationship of resemblance and difference.

M. STORTI / O. DELACOUR: And what about the problem of food in all this?

L. IRIGARAY: In mothering, food often takes the place of language. Instead of providing you with words and images as well, I only give you food. And we could also wonder about the relationship between this function of a mute wet nurse and a consumer society. Behind all this, isn't there the relation to some woman who gives herself to others as food and leaves them to blindly consume her? This explains children's problems with food, as well as other problems...

M. STORTI / O. DELACOUR: In *And One Doesn't Stir Without the Other* you express the desire for a real duality between a mother and her daughter, for them both to be free and autonomous subjects. How is this possible, all the more so since our mothers often refuse to discuss things when we talk to them about sexuality for example...

L. IRIGARAY: Of course, it's not always easy. It happens very slowly. We ourselves hesitate, and our mothers don't respond right away. So many taboos still weigh on such exchanges. It's never too late to lift them. But to talk to one's mother as a woman presupposes saying goodbye to an all-powerful mother, accepting that one's mother isn't the all-protector, the ultimate amorous recourse, the refuge against abandonment. This allows for establishing ties of reciprocity with her through which she will eventually be able to feel like my daughter. It's not easy. What strikes me is how impossible it is practically for a daughter to give up on her mother. As if the death of one were the death of the other.

M. STORTI / O. DELACOUR: Because a mother isn't just anyone. She's someone who gave me life, who fed me, with whom I had my first physical contact.

L. IRIGARAY: Yes, but this relationship is most often lived passively and silently. It lacks exchanges, gestures and words which would leave, and even provide, each woman her own life mobility.

M. STORTI / O. DELACOUR: So, wouldn't we have to substitute "free us from mothers" for "free us from fathers"?

L. IRIGARAY: No, but rather: "Let's free ourselves with our mothers." This is an essential condition for our emancipation from the authority of fathers. As long as there aren't harmonious relations between daughters and mothers, mothers and daughters — between women — the father is the one who will then impose "order" — no matter how repressive — into this dark and passionate relationship. By claiming the monopoly of divine right…. The mother/daughter, daughter/mother relationship is an extremely explosive nucleus in our societies. Conceiving it and changing it amounts to disturbing the patriarchal order. Women's movements have been turning around this issue and are only just starting to broach it.

21

M. STORTI / O. DELACOUR: It's fashionable to be anti-feminist today, to say "feminism is over," what do you think about this?

L. IRIGARAY: Just as we've consumed women, now we're consuming the end of women's struggles. It's fashionable, certain people need to find out what the trends are, what's going to work for the media. So feminism is over? I think it's much more accurate to say women's struggles have only just begun. As for the word feminism, who can say? Isn't it a new burden to bear? Yet another *ism* that fuels ugly arguments and undermines our cause?

M. STORTI / O. DELACOUR: Alright, but today we're in a paradoxical situation: on the one hand, women's activities have multiplied these past few years. We're starting to do what we didn't do (or only did a little bit) before, and on a large scale. At the same time, there's a feeling of crisis, of difficulties in continuing certain kinds of struggles and in making progress. This is so widespread that recovery into a reformist, egalitarian, almost official "feminism," is itself becoming a common occurrence.

L. IRIGARAY: First, there are obvious social realities. There are many who want people to say: "Enough with women's struggles!" The economic crisis, unemployment, the falling birth rate bring along with them a certain type of discourse like: "Go back home and keep quiet." So, we should ask ourselves whether the internal "crisis" of the "movement" isn't prescribed by the general socio-economic crisis and whether women are sufficiently analyzing these determinations. Maybe the "movement" should turn more towards society as a whole, interpret what's going on there, and find out what action is appropriate now. Paradoxically, although it's collective, the movement sometimes was too individualistic. It hasn't reflected enough about its own social, economic and political dimensions. And, when it did, it often followed models of struggles that weren't specific to women.

Personal problems are all too rarely informed by socio-economic questions. For women, however, private and public struggles are indissociable. Dividing them doesn't make sense. But it suits other people fine... Furthermore, in times of crisis, some social strata suffer more than others. Women, for example... When there's an "emergency," their problems once again are repressed, put aside, buried under apparently more pressing realities. Is this the reason for the oscillations in the history of women? Women emerge, then disappear again? Shouldn't they learn to guard themselves from bearing the brunt of crises? And also from having everything that's not going right projected onto them — an age-old mechanism we should be able to decipher very quickly now. But something among us circulates much too much: pessimism and guilt. The fear of not being "pure" enough or of coming up against dead ends, as if all stuggles and governments haven't run into dead ends. Do they lower their heads just for that or do they shamelessly proclaim that everything's going for the better? We really should free ourselves from shame, and also be more assertive and more on the attack. The movement has often responded reactively to events. Maybe it was unavoidable at one time, but now it's time to move into another stage. And also learn to anticipate them...

M. STORTI / O. DELACOUR: But as for us, we're dying from our "crises" and our "dead ends." And even so, we've got to recognize that some attacks against feminism or the women's movement wouldn't be made today if they didn't rely on elements of "truth." You mentioned the defensive aspect of the movement, we could also say that it has been institutionalized. This isn't only true of women's movements, but also of "leftism" in general. Let's say that we've reproduced what we were fighting against.

L. IRIGARAY: It's true that there hasn't been enough of a clean break with institutions. There can be an incredible nostalgia for "going back home" behind the desire to publish a great journal, become a self-sufficient publishing house, get such-and-such a job, or sometimes even to get married and have kids. Once again, the weight of institutions has been underestimated. But it could also be said that women haven't cared enough about creating relays, relations, new ways of organizing themselves. I already mentioned the need to re-establish our descent and ascent with our mothers, our grandmothers, and our entire cultural and militant past that does exist and that our "masters" never taught us to know. But there's also the confinement in groups, cities, social classes, countries… Of course networks are already in operation, but they should be reinforced and the efforts should be delocalized. We have much to teach each other, and also much encouragement and support to give each other. Is acting a certain way out-of-date today? Maybe. Who cares? So many others are just getting started. It's rather amusing that people dare bury women's struggles. They've never existed in so many places and in so many different forms. These remarks come from blasé intellectual circles, among others, that are always eager for the next new thing. Are women today really less enslaved by society?

M. STORTI / O. DELACOUR: Let's take a specific example, abortion. In the entire world there's a regression or at least a movement towards regression in the number of people who support its legalization, specifically in the U.S.A. and in Europe. In France, the National Assembly will once again "pore over" this issue in the fall. At this very moment, attacks are coming from all sides. Political parties are settling their electoral disagreements, notably on the occasion of the European elections, on women's bellies. There is still very little mobilization against it, even if discussions and meetings are being resumed. But women who already mobilized five years ago or more aren't too enthusiastic about having to start over.

L. IRIGARAY: Of course, we have to take up the campaigns and actions again — expand them, internationalize them. It's tedious to keep asking for the same rights over and over again — basic rights really. And it's tedious to keep answering the same questions, to clear up the same misunderstandings, to deny the motives people ascribe to us. It's also tiresome to reaffirm that it's not about forbidding or dissuading women from having children, but rather it's about allowing them to have the children they can or want to have — without being penalized both legally and economically in the image of themselves that society throws back at them.

Do we have to say it all again – what patience it takes – that no woman is ever happy about getting an abortion; that she "forgets" to take the pill because she doesn't feel like she's valued in her sexual life; that for centuries, her stomach, her body, her pleasure haven't been worth anything unless they were subjected to reproduction and mothering. We shouldn't simply fight to get laws passed, so that they should be applied and enforced, but also make sure they're suitable and bearable for women. How many women have gone to get karmized in solitude and anguish owing to the ratification of the Veil law?[2] And at a high price.

M. STORTI / O. DELACOUR: Beyond abortion and contraception lies sexuality. You were one of the first to encour-

25

age women to create their own sexuality. But groups don't talk about it much...

L. IRIGARAY: We still don't talk enough among ourselves about sexual issues. Every time we meet up, namely to address problems concerning contraception and abortion, it would be useful for us to talk about our sexuality, to share our problems, to understand how our desires underwent an abortion in our girlhood and continue to be aborted in our lives as women. Simply having the courage to relate the difficulty we met in fulfilling our desires, our pleasure, our loves, makes these things less dramatic. But here again, let's not remain reactive... discovering the imagination and the language of our desires positively is much more fascinating. We're not going to wait once again for competent men, doctors, sexologists, to teach us a lesson. Or even let our mothers be accused of having supported fascism. Were they in power? Did they have a say in choosing the government? So, we might as well admit it that the entire patriarchal system which doesn't leave women any other function or worth than maternity, is potentially fascist – and that some patriarchs have benefited from this and will continue to do so.

M. STORTI / O. DELACOUR: These would just be secondary benefits resulting from oppression...

L. IRIGARAY: Oppression coming from difference that's functioning hierarchically. Difference exists. Difference in race, difference in tradition, difference in class, difference in gender... How can we refuse or deny that? The problem is that difference has always been a means for subordination and slavery. But affirming difference has nothing to do with some kind of racism, on the contrary. It's lifting from the masters their right to decree laws for every man and woman, at all times and in all places — because these supposedly universal laws are really just the laws of a system that's in power, the laws of the "strongest." No doubt, you have to be among the "weakest" in order to see the repressive nature of such laws. When women ask for the right to difference, they are asking not to be subjugated to masculine or, more precisely, patriarchal models that paralyze and negate them in their sexual, social and cultural station. Why is there so much resistance to hearing about it as well? Is it a deliberate deafness, meant to preserve the established order? Is it a consequence of age-old repression and censorship? Or is it an effect of... difference?

2

IF DAUGHTER AND MOTHER
SPOKE TO EACH OTHER

MARYSE MARTY: Who are you?

LUCE IRIGARAY: I'm French even though I was born in Belgium of a mother who's part French and a half Italian father. Irigaray is my married name. I've lived in Paris since 1960. My present job is: Director of Research in Philosophy at the CNRS.[3] I'm a trained psychoanalyst. I've studied many subjects (philosophy, humanities, linguistics, literature) and written 15 books that have been translated into various languages.

For about 20 years now, I've devoted most of my life to thinking and practicing a new historical era where women can exist and reflect upon what they are in respect to their difference(s) with men. It's an exciting and very difficult task; it comes up against much suffering, enthusiasm, and resistances too. I still think that I am and always will be "on the barricades." Actually, I don't think only when I'm working at a desk, I also think when I meet with women, many women, especially abroad, but also in France. I work with mixed circles as well, both scientific and political. Every day I ask myself questions, I look for my own path, my truth: between past, present and future. Nature is a great retreat for me when relations with men and women are too painful, too tiring. I was raised in the Christian Catholic tradition: I've suffered from it and I've been blessed by it, I've met men and women who are exceptional in their freedom and in their friendship: to name a few, Father Chenu, some people belonging to the *Esprit*[4] groups, and, more recently, some women from the ACGF.[5] I learned how to understand my tradition by listening to what it has become in the lives of men and women who practice it outside of any strict obedience: maybe they don't go to Mass, but they know how to love and respect. Practicing yoga and opening up to Far-Eastern traditions, namely the Indian tradition, also shed another light, another breath, on the words and gestures that were passed on to me through the Old and New Testaments, and also through reading the Koran.

M. MARTY: Why is this issue of mother-daughter relationships so topical?

L. IRIGARAY: There are several reasons. It's difficult to know which one comes first or foremost. Our age is very interested in psychological issues and we've discovered that there are often serious and painful problems between daughters and mothers. It's generally the daughters who talk about it, at least in certain instances. In my work as a psychoanalyst, I've almost never heard a woman talk to me about difficult relations with her mother without getting upset. But all the suffering in many women's lives comes from something that never blossomed in their relationship with their mother. I've also heard it from my friends and women I've met on various occasions, namely in the struggles for women's liberation. These struggles have significantly helped women become aware of themselves, and this helped shed some light on the "dark continent" of the daughter's relationship with the mother that Freud talked about. Women's liberation corresponds first to women's taking the floor, to reciprocal listening and to the discovery of truths that weren't spoken or known as long as women were isolated from each other. Thanks to women's coming together, to the trust that can exist between them, hidden realities have come out in the open. Among them is the suffering that exists in the daughter to mother relationship. This suffering doesn't mean that everything is negative; most often there are good moments, moments of complicity, but something crucial is missing: communication with the mother, both close and at a distance, and this is something the daughter can't let go of.

M. MARTY: Why is this so important?

L. IRIGARAY: It's an opportunity for women to find their own way again: both individually and together. Suffering in relation to the mother is often expressed as a break between an almost natural intimacy and a lack of understanding, a lack of personal exchanges. It seems to go without saying that daughters and mothers are in agreement with each other, and, at the same time, they remain strangers. They're accomplices on some level, blind to each other on another. And even their complicity irritates the daughter, as if it were expressing an obligation to do and to be like their mother. In responses that I received to a survey cue asking people to make a sentence with the words "mother-daughter," there were many sentences like "the mother and daughter look alike," "like mother, like daughter," but this resemblance didn't always seem to please the daughters. It provoked ambiguous feelings in them, namely because resemblance is imposed on them from the outside. Often for the daughter, on some level, there's only one path available to her: get married and have children like her mother, even if she's "liberated" elsewhere, if she works for instance. The daughter wants to become like her mother and, at the same time, is repulsed by this idea because this "do like" is imposed on her and doesn't give her any worth as a unique person with a unique story. All women should resemble each other, except for some flaws or familial qualities, whereas men should be encouraged to assert themselves, make their mark, open new paths, suggest new models... But to have to resemble someone, to have to do and be like someone, doesn't make for interesting exchanges between two people but rather for wild passions, stifling complicities, and infinite loves and hates. These blind passions and complicities are often linked to the fact that daughters and mothers have the same body: they talk about the corporal events that mark their life: puberty, pregnancy, childbirth, breastfeeding, mothering children... They talk about it as women, in collusion in regard to the men's world, but often they're still lacking a personal path for exchange. Each one's story lacks words and images, and their spiritual journey is the same once again —often a little vague or abstract — because it's defined by a universe in the masculine and this universe doesn't provide representations that valorize the important moments in a woman's life. In order for daughter and mother to communicate, they need words, images, symbols which represent the significant events in their life and which allow to build them in the feminine. I remember the joy I experienced at the Torcello Museum when I discovered that a beautiful statue I was looking at didn't represent Mary and Jesus as is most often the case, but rather Anne presenting me her daughter Mary, who was sitting on her knees. We lack these kinds of markers for navigating through the history of the relationship with our mother. We also need these markers in order to have successful relationships with other women: our mothers, sisters or spiritual daughters.

M. MARTY: Have things always been this way?

L. IRIGARAY: No, they haven't. The ancient wooden statue at Torcello proves it: statues and paintings representing Anne and Mary are more often found in museums than in our churches today (and, on another level, the virgin of Lourdes is most often seen without Bernadette…). Many women don't even know that this popular form of worship existed and still exists in certain regions and certain cultures: to give two examples, Brittany and the Canadian Indians. Other cultures attest to the existence of spiritual relationships between mothers and daughters: thus, one of the originary couples of the Greek gods' families is the great goddess Demeter and her daughter Kore. The story of their separation by the god of the underworld, who takes the daughter from her mother in order to marry her by force, is an enlightening story that's still topical in some way. You can read about it in Clémence Ramnoux's *Mythologie, ou la famille olympienne* [Mythology, or the Olympian Family] and in the last chapter of my book *Thinking the Difference*: "The Forgotten Mystery of Feminine Genealogies." You'll find that, at that time, Demeter made the entire earth sterile until her daughter was returned, and she had to force the god of gods, Zeus, to intervene for this to happen. As for relationships between daughters and mothers, the discovery of each relationship can be informed by other women's stories, certainly, but it can also be informed by our pre-history, which often enlightens us on women's history, as Freud himself says. What he doesn't say, however, is that the culture of relationships between daughter and mother turns their meeting with the other gender into a *something-more* and not a *something-less* for women.

M. MARTY: How can the culture of relationships between daughter and mother promote a better relationship between women and men?

L. IRIGARAY: The masculine world appears then like another world with which it's possible to establish a fertile alliance, not only naturally but spiritually as well. The father and the husband no longer represent the law necessary for the little girl, for the woman, to raise herself above simple nature. Man represents the other that's irreducible to me, the cultural partner, the love partner with whom body and words are united in a relationship.

For the daughter, discovering a relationship of words with her mother corresponds to discovering the path of her incarnation as a woman: the path of the relationship inside herself between body and words. So, the woman is no longer the nature-body for which man will be the words, she is no longer the flesh for which man will be the word: both woman and man are a different body and different words, and, because of this, they can unite their incarnations and engender spiritual as well as natural children, the first ones becoming the cradle where the second ones will be received. I think that such an alliance between women and men could work towards achieving the reign of the spirit which, according to Christian theology, corresponds to our present mission.

M. MARTY: Why do mothers talk about their daughters and not vice versa?

L. IRIGARAY: I think I already gave a reason for this common and strange occurrence: daughters' suffering is often silent, still wordless, guilty. Mothers are in the stronger position, they're more protected. They "have" the daughters about whom they talk; as for the daughters, they "are" only daughters, the mother isn't their property like the daughter is for the mother. In addition to this, mothers have done so many things for their daughters: carry them, give birth to them, feed them, mother them... They always have positive things to say about them, as well as about themselves, which allows for the more negative things to be left in the dark. As for the daughter, she likes or doesn't like her mother. It's not always easy to say. She has to like her, it's a duty. If things were less simple, how could mothers talk about them? In addition to this, the daughter, once again, lacks the distance to have words about the mother. She's in a dual relationship with her that's made up of body and affects, without a culture that allows for a perspective on the relationship. Sometimes it's only after the birth of her first child that she can think about her mother. As for the mother, she has a husband, kids, a job maybe... Talking about her daughter is contextualized by life, putting things at a distance is much easier, and also more conventional. The mother talks about her daugher in the framework of a micro-society: the family. The daughter lives the relationship to her mother as a relationship between two people where one has a valorized role, the mother, and the other doesn't: her. In this interview, I'm trying to let the daughter speak, as I've already done on other occasions, namely in a short work: *And One Doesn't Move Without the Other,* where the daughter addresses her mother to tell her about both her distress and her love.

M. MARTY: Can paying attention to the mother-daughter relationship have an effect on our way of speaking?

L. IRIGARAY: Yes. Paying attention to the mother-daughter relationship can change our relationship to words for the better on two accounts. First, by leading us to respect the exceptional capacity for dialogue exhibited by the words of the little girl to her mother, and also by not forgetting that this is the place where the relationship between two *she's* exists and can be cultivated or canceled. The little girl addresses her mother by saying: "Mom, do you want to come and play with me?," "Mom, I'm tired. Are you?," "Mom, can I brush your hair?," etc. In these words there's always an *I* and a *you* in dialogue who live or do something together. This relation of words between the little girl and her mother is unique: it goes from the daughter towards the mother. It's unique because we don't see it in any other situation, except in the nostalgia of adults, both women and men. Men make the same kind of sentences when they are asked to imagine a little girl's words to her mother. As for the little boy, on the other hand, he, both in reality and in adults' sentences, says: "I want to play ball," or "I'd like to play ball," or "Come play ball." There's no longer two people talking to each other even if sometimes they do something together, playing for instance. Unfortunately, for the most part, the mother uses the imperative when she talks to her daughter (canceling out the dialogue between *I* and *you* that the daughter respects by using the interrogative). "Clean up your things if you want to watch TV," "Get some milk on your way home from school," or she talks about the relations between them in the "do like" way: "I acted just like you when I was little," "I went through that too" (menstruation, for instance). So, the mother no longer respects the two poles of dialogue: *I* and *you*, unless sometimes, often even, when she's talking to the boy: "Do you want me to come kiss you in your bed?" This is one of the explanations for the daughter's silence and suffering. Another explanation is that, from grammar school on, and even before, the feminine *you* of the mother is going to be erased by a society or culture in the masculine: he, they [*ils*] (even in mixed situations: the parents, for example, or the *she* of the mother disappears in the *they, them* [*ils, eux*]).

M. MARTY: Does the suffering go beyond the daughter's suffering?

L. IRIGARAY: The little girl has the greatest aptitude for dialogue; she wants to talk *with*, and, first *with her*, her mother. Strangely enough, our tradition is deaf to this demand, at least today: the little girl doesn't even find a *with Her*, the Mother, with whom to have an innner dialogue. This is painful for the daughter or the woman, and paralyzes their becoming in communication with themselves and with others. It's also a loss for the entire culture, for all community life: a loss of dialogues, of exchanges between people, a loss of feminine identity, of fruitfulness, of the difference between woman and man: I_{she} and you_{he}, I_{he} and you_{she}. Actually if I_{she} became an impersonal I_{one}, dialogue respectful of difference, with the masculine partner or partners, would become impossible. It's the same way for the inner path of I_{she} and the building of real, unconventional or simply affective relationships between women: I_{she} and you_{she} are covered up by other norms of exchanges. These norms are often more abstract or are sustained by exchanging objects or money more than by an exchange between people themselves.

M. MARTY: What impact does the lack of a culture based in the relationship between daughter and mother, mother and daughter, have on a woman's social status?

L. IRIGARAY: The woman can't maintain her woman's identity in society without the possibility of returning to her, to I_{she}: she disappears, remains silent, plays the man, changes into *one*,… If she doesn't have memory, images or words reminding her that she is I_{she}, she can't represent herself as *she*, a woman, nor can she represent other women as women. I think re-finding her feminine I is essential for both presenting and representing herself as for being able to meet and represent other women in collective life. It's a long haul that's opening before us. It's worth the trouble…

THE SEXUATION
OF LANGUAGE

Concerning *Speaking Is Never Neutral* (*Parler n'est jamais neutre*, 1985) and certain chapters of *Sexes and Genders through Languages* (*Sexes et genres à travers les langues*, 1987).

"Luce Irigaray and the Difference Between the Sexes" (*Le Monde,* June 7, 1985) and "Do We Speak to Each Other in the Feminine?" (*Paris Féministe,* 116, March 1991).

3

THE DIFFERENCE BETWEEN THE SEXES

ROGER-POL DROIT: Women's struggles, analysis of schizophrenics' discourse, psychoanalytic interpretations of philosophers, call for new values... How do these all fit together? There must be a link that reveals the coherence of an approach that, at first, seems fragmented, even contradictory.

Speaking is Never Neutral, your last book, contains fourteen studies written from 1966 to 1982, and four unpublished studies. It questions how messages are elaborated, how they are rooted in the sexed body of speaking beings, and in their powers: "A word is as good as a chemical product. But it has its toxins... A discourse can poison, surround, corner, imprison or liberate, heal, nourish, fertilize. It is rarely neutral."

Your reflection is based on investigations. Several chapters on psycholinguistics summarize experimental research you conducted for over twenty years on the discourse of "disturbed" and "normal" subjects. They tend to prove that none of us use language identically, as a simple code shared by everyone, a set of neutral tools allegedly meant to communicate — some better than others maybe — in a uniform way. In what seems to be the most trivial conversation, everybody unknowingly would mobilize the structure of his/her relationship to language, to others, and to the world. How do you prove this? By changing the focus from "utterances" (*énon-*

41

cés) to "enunciation." How do you differentiate "utterance" from "enunciation"?

LUCE IRIGARAY: Roughly speaking, you would separate what's already said, written, recorded, etc., from what is being said here and now.

Utterances refer to messages that have already been produced, finished, that are like dead, if you put aside the meaning they retain in their final form.

Enunciation, on the other hand, designates speech as it unfolds, its live, actual engendering, not yet stabilized. Linguists generally deal with utterances, or with ideal schemes allegedly spoken by everyone (or by any speaker in a given language). Any attempt to elaborate a grammar of enunciation should show how speech, meaning, and communication are engendered and brought about through the subject's psyche, his/her story, his/her relationship to the world and the other.

I have studied this production in specific corpuses. I listened, recorded, and interpreted them in order to show empirically how different types of enunciation exist, how the material, the situation, the subjects and their relationships bring about different morphologies in a state of becoming.

R.-P. DROIT: There's still a problem. You say that enunciation is creative, not fixed. But the examples you use, on the contrary, show that the subjects — whether hysterical, obssessive or schizophrenic — repeat types of utterances which betray a fixed position in relation to discourse, as if there was a model beneath their enunciation. What then?

L. IRIGARAY: Many of us repeat already formed, programmed utterances. But any pathology, whether individual or social, can be defined that way. Our psychism is like a soil for cultivating messages. It would keep producing if we cultivated it to go on creating. If our psychism doesn't create new forms, if it manifests no originality, it proves to be sick, corpse-like, fossilized. This is where the major interest of psychoanalysis lies: the way it deals with speech presents a unique, experimental situation of enunciation. It allows someone to listen to and release one's psyche by reshaping discourse.

Actually, the possible openings of someone's discourse are inscribed in the forms of his/her messages and not in their explicit content. The patient doesn't know and can't possibly know what (s)he's saying. Hence the need for another to help one orient and identify oneself.

R.-P. DROIT: The specific *mise en scène* of psychoanalysis —several chapters of the book deal with it — allows the subject to confront his/her speech. As if, on the couch, the patient was progressively coming to terms with the mystery of language itself, this paradox of speech where what (s)he says, according to the rules of lexicon and syntax, incessantly contradicts what (s)he wants to say. As if speaking consisted in groping towards the horizon of one's desire through a web of words and the order of language. Is this approach the same for men and women?

L. IRIGARAY: No. Listening rigorously to various discourses led me to discover that language is sexed. Only part of this ongoing investigation can be found in *Speaking is Never Neutral*.

Women don't have the same relationship as men do to the other and to the world and they don't translate it into discourse in the same way. I'm talking about a different generation of messages, not about adding or eliminating a few words.

This fact is denied by men and women who follow Freud and practice his teaching, even though Freud became an analyst by listening to the aberrant singularity of language traveling through the body of his female patients. Language called "hysterical" creates circuits that are somatic since theyre not expressed in words: this discovery is outlined in *Studies on Hysteria*, but Freud seems to forget it after *The Interpretation of Dreams*. He listens to his first female patients, he learns something. He doesn't listen to Dora, for example, and forces his masculine schemes over her. She's right to leave him, she can't say anything. He shuts her mouth, in various ways... By then the analysis of Dora is nothing but "the Freud case."

Based on a sexual pathology, psychoanalysis today refuses the sexuation of those who participate in the analytic scene. It ratifies the neutering of the sexual element which goes together with the imperialism of monocratic discourse and the technological age, its ultimate achievement.

R.-P. DROIT: You're aware that asserting the existence of a sexed language meets strong resistances...

L. IRIGARAY: I am. But why aren't these resistances interpreted in light of psychoanalysis, which is supposed to interpret and remove social and moral repressions? This is quite surprising.

These resistances bring about aberrations, especially scientific ones, which would be rather amusing if they didn't express the despair of our time. We have no problem accepting that the brain is sexed, but not language. Are we saying that we're speaking independently of our brain? Which part of us does? What role would the brain play when we speak? Can part of us stay asexed? Should we or can we accept that sexuality can't be translated into verbal, symbolic, or aesthetic forms? Aren't those who deny or refuse the sexuation of discourse *de facto* accomplices in the repression of sexuality?

R.-P. DROIT: The sexual liberation of the past twenty years, despite some positive effects, has led to quite a few snares, false appearances, and impasses. Do you think that another liberation is possible?

L. IRIGARAY: Experience has proven that the often mechanical language of pornography doesn't interest everybody, and not all the time. Many men, and women especially, are ready to "reintegrate their home" without having fully developed their libido. They are driven back into another era of repression.

The world can't afford the luxury of this repression anymore. It needs sexual difference not just in order to reproduce, but to be revived and produce a new culture.

Sexual liberation doesn't simply mean the demand for sexual equality. Even though sexual equality is socially positive, it runs the risk of producing monosexed, neutralized crowds, and this is one of the dangers of our time. Sexual liberation is more about making a non-hierarchized difference come into being, a difference that allows for the creation of various imaginary, symbolic, and artistic forms that are consistent with the sexes and are productive in their differences.

R.-P. DROIT: If "speaking is never neutral," scientific discourse isn't neutral either. The subject of science, which doesn't say "I," "you," or "we" — which seems to be sexless — would be in some way be a masked man who forgets that his "objective" research is actually bound to his sexual imagination. It wouldn't be a question of falling back into some sterile subjectivism, but moreso a question of making scientific thought conscious of the soil where it originates. And this may not be that easy. If scientific neutrality is unknowingly masculine, then what kind of science is still possible?

L. IRIGARAY: Quite a strange question! A feminine science seems impossible to you? A science conscious of the subject that elaborates it would no longer be a science? Or would it be a science without subjective or objective control, one that's aware of the language-tool it's using? A sexed science would be able to create new forms of truth, and also new forms of beauty and wisdom. This happens at the beginning of every historical era and we need it in order to exist in our world, instead of limiting ourselves to exploiting it efficiently.

Science can't be separated from an ethical concern. Our sexed bodies resist the dispersion and disintegration which threaten us at the end of this technological and scientific era. They probably are the only safe place in us and between us, protected from the blind and polemical powers that threaten to destroy all life with a slight of hand.

These words don't compromise with the facts, they are scientific and, ethically, realistic.

4

Do We Speak to Each Other in the Feminine?

ODETTE BRUN: In its February 15, 1991 issue, Paris Féministe reopened an important debate for our becoming-women: sexed distinctions in language raised by the "Feminine-Masculine Dictionary of Professions, Titles, and Electoral Functions" put together by women of francophone Switzerland. You have been dealing with this aspect of women's — and men's — liberation for years with teams of female and male researchers who have come together to address this problem. The majority of the French media turn a deaf ear on these studies, studies that particularly affect us. In your last two books (*Je Tu Nous* and *Sexes and Genealogies*) you conclude from the answers to short linguistic tests that women and men don't speak in the same way. Actually, you're not the only woman to demonstrate this. For this study, you gathered together women and men of different languages and cultures who analyze and comment upon the answers you collected, especially in *Sexes and Genealogies*. Which sample are you and your research group working on right now?

LUCE IRIGARAY: The number of answers collected at this point for the cues discussed in *Sexes and Genealogies* amounts to about 500 for women and 350 for men (not counting those collected in Canada — about 350 — which I only partially use). The total number of answers in foreign languages is at least 1000 for women and 800 for men (they're always more reticent...).[6]

O. BRUN: Women and men don't speak in the same way. This would explain quite a few of their conflicts or misunderstandings, including love and also politics. Can you give examples of differences in speech between women and men?

L. IRIGARAY: Men are much more apt to be the subjects of their own speech. Even when it comes to making a sentence with one or several words belonging to the feminine world, they try to say *I* [*je*]. When told to make a sentence with the words *robe-se-voir* [dress-oneself-see],[7] men will make answers like: "I don't see myself in a dress" or "He already sees himself in his lawyer's gown." Even when their sentence is "She is seen in a dress," the man is still the subject... It means: *she* is visible in a dress (by me, a man), and not: she is seen by herself in a dress. Example: "She is seen from afar in her dress" [*Elle se voit de loin avec sa robe*] doesn't have the same real subject of "see," as: "She thinks she looks beautiful in her Sunday dress" [*Elle se voit belle dans sa robe du dimanche*]. Men remain in the logic of their *I* whereas women have difficulty affirming themselves as subjects. They erase themselves by saying "one" (*on*)[8] or by using the *infinitive*: "One looks good in a mirror wearing a dress" [*On se voit bien en robe dans un miroir*], "Seeing oneself in a dress is pleasing" [*Se voir en robe est agréable*]. For them, the *I* often times is still the man's, hence it's not uncommon to get sentences such as "Those (masculine plural) that I see wearing dresses are beautiful" or sentences that show that if the woman puts on a dress, it's in order to be seen by a man: "She is putting on her dress to go see him tonight." The great deficiency in women's language is "she" [*elle*], the other woman: mother, daughter or sister (I use these words in the real or figural sense).

It's not only the fashion to wear pants that brings about these answers. If you ask men and women to make a sentence with words like: "dog" [*chien*] or even "child" [*enfant*], answers show that 85% of men and 75% of women use a male subject for the word "dog." There are a few more feminine subjects for the word "child," but much less than one would think. And when a woman is the subject of the sentence, the action is most likely to be expressed by: feed, rock, wash... whereas the man: loves, plays with, cares about, etc. When asked to make a sentence with "mother," men usually refer to their own mother rather than to their wife as a mother, and a cue word like "femininity" or "pregnancy" elicits sentences like "I'm cultivating my relation with femininity" or "How could a man live through pregnancy?"

O. BRUN: What about the way people talk to each other?

L. IRIGARAY: The answers go in the same direction as before. For the cue: "worry–to him/to her" [*lui–tell*], men will talk among themselves about their worries: "I tell him/her my worries." To whom? Most often to a male friend, to a professor, etc. Very rarely to a woman, unless they complain to her as to a mother. And women? Women talk to very few "her(s)," very few talk "among themselves" [*entre elles*]. They generally tell their problems to Jim, John, a husband, a professor. It's true that *lui* ["to him/to her"] is a term marked by the masculine gender...

O. BRUN: Have you tried to use cues that are less gendered?

L. IRIGARAY: Yes. For example, I told them to make a sentence with the reflexive word *se* (which can also be understood as *ce* [masculine singular demonstrative pronoun meaning "this, that"] or *ceux* [masculine plural demonstrative pronoun meaning "those"].[9] Without hesitation, men will make a sentence saying: "He scratches himself" [*Il se gratte*], "He takes a walk" [*Il se promène*], "He bought himself a car" [*Il s'est acheté une voiture*], etc. Women, on the other hand, will make a sentence more linked to a context or will stick to the neutral. They don't yet think "in the feminine." We find very few answers with *elle se* but more with *il se* and sentences using the demonstrative pronoun *ce*, a more frequent choice by women from more modest or less cultivated backgrounds: "This garden is blooming" [*Ce jardin est fleuri*], "The dress that Christine is wearing this morning" [*La robe que porte Christine ce matin*].

O. BRUN: Have you used cue words that address relationships dealing with friendship or love between people?

L. IRIGARAY: Among many other examples, we asked various groups to write what the words "they love each other" [*ils s'aiment*] brought to mind. The most frequent answers are: "Arthur and Mary love each other," "the lovers love each other," "two people love each other." More often men will say "He loves himself" or "They love each other for life" [*Ils s'aiment pour la vie*] (without putting emphasis on the two partners). But the big surprise is the meaning given to *elles s'aiment* ["they love each other" in the feminine]. Around half of the answers are of the kind: "Elle sème..."[10] ["She sows..." "wheat" or "disorder"]. Another symptom: men express a rejection of the relationships between women: "They love each other, the bitches" [*Elles s'aiment les salopes*].

We have also found that men often put their words in the past tense whereas women express themselves most often in the present or future. It's probably due to the fact that men relate their words, images and thoughts to a context already defined by their culture. They're more at ease in their language, in their references to meaning, and they move within it by using "time" [*le temps*]: especially between the present and the past, a backtracking of sorts. Women, on the other hand, are generally searching for a path: from words that they know and their daily surroundings. But their words, which are closer to life, are paralyzed by existing rules and customs, for example the rule that requires that the masculine is to be used in all mixed situations: *ils,*[11] or that human kind is represented by *il*, etc. The imperialist privilege of the *il(s)* is fairly unconscious and weighs heavy.

O. BRUN: Can you give other examples of this (quite imperialist...) weight of the *il(s)*?

L. IRIGARAY: The unconscious weight or authority of the *il* [he] over the *elle* [she] and the ideological connotations accompanying the *elle* can be seen in two very different types of texts: the scientific text and the literary text. Examples chosen by an eminent linguist like Chomsky to illustrate demonstration are practically always in the masculine: John or Bill, Jim or Tom, are not-sexually-neutral characters he uses to illustrate proofs that have a scientific or universal aim. If the feminine comes into play, it's in sentences such as "I found a secretary who will do the job," "I demand a secretary that my colleagues can appreciate," "She thinks this man is a great scientist" (Maurice Gross, *Grammaire transformationnelle du français*). If you look at the novels of Marguerite Yourcenar and Marguerite Duras — *L'Œuvre au noir* and *L'Amour*[12] — which I chose because they were at hand that day, they show that, out of twice two pages of text, the characters are, for Marguerite Yourcenar, 95% he's and 4% she's and, for Marguerite Duras, 95% he's and 5% she's. Who would have believed it? And, when women appear in their works, it's in situations of prostitution, murder, incest (cf. *Feux* and *Anna soror*[13] by Marguerite Yourcenar) or as objects that are seen, desired or possessed by a man (in Marguerite Duras). It's obviously not enough to be a woman in order to conceive and create as a woman in our age... At least in a non-traditional way.

O. BRUN: Does this mean that, on a certain level, after twenty years of struggles and victories, women haven't yet changed their way of understanding the world, others, and themselves?

L. IRIGARAY: Social changes are not merely the same as identity changes. The constitution of the deeper self necessarily comes into being with language, images, and representations. And so far, not much has evolved in these domains. Awareness and the so-called women's liberation are still inscribed in a cultural geography that's almost entirely masculine. In the familial context, women were bullied but supported by their immediate surroundings, which were more their own. It's not about going backwards. But we have to understand that women of today enter into a social outside without that outside's accepting or welcoming them as women. Even if women become very "active" on the current job market, their internal exile remains. They have to face a double me: remain traditional women at home (most often the case...) and become quasi-men outside the home. Many lose themselves between arrogance (including in relation to other women) and more or less self-proclaimed personal distress. Doesn't society as it stands set a trap for women: you "will have" a bit more on the condition that you "be" a bit less? Being faced with dilemmas like these, it's time for women to react and come up with solutions that suit their identity as women. Changing language is one such solution.

O. BRUN: In your last seminar I learned that it wasn't enough to say *I*-subject. This *I* must be sexed, I have to say *I*-woman. Personally, as a child, I learned to say *I*-myself which was marked, as my generation has been, by a masculine assumed to be neuter (humankind). I'm not sure my *I* is always an *I*-woman. Thank you for helping me, for helping us with this.

THE SYMBOLIC ORDER: HISTORY, PHILOSOPHY, RELIGION

Concerning the *Inchiesta* issue: *Il Divino concepito da noi (1990)* and the relationships between history and philosophy.

From: "Jesus's Relationship to Female Aboriginal Traditions" (*Il Manifesto,* July 3,1990) and "Historical Perspectives" (*Expresso,* July, 1991)

5

A Bridge Between Two Irreducible to Each Other

ROSELLA BOFIGLIOLI: Each individual's access to rational maturity comes about through the interpretation of religious and civic mythologies in their historical unfolding. Can you explain a bit more about how it's possible to fix the boundaries of a new relationship between these two realms, the civic and the religious, taking into consideration our current political climate, especially the crisis and reflection on what claims to be the "Left?"

LUCE IRIGARAY: First, it seems necessary to define what belongs to the civic sphere and what belongs to the religious sphere, in ourselves as well as in the society in which we live. This isn't an easy task because it requires distancing oneself from one's affects, beliefs and also one's deeper, more obscure ties. It demands all at the same time autoconsciousness in solitude, analyzing relationships with others — women and men — interpretation of current mythologies, those past and even those to come. Secondly, I think that, in our day and age, it's necessary to put civic choice before religious choice. Our plurireligious and international society needs civic laws meant for all women and men, which would guarantee one's self-respect as a real person, respect of others and of the community in general, and of the management of its possessions (natural, material, spiritual). I also think the religious objective would have to change from a "cult" of adoration — idolatrist, blind? — for a God generally designated in the masculine, an all powerful and corporally absent God, towards the spiritualization of our living bodies, especially in the way we love nature, ourselves, our fellow humans and the other half of the human genus: those (masculine or feminine) who are different from us. This means, among other things, that one task for our time is to establish a horizontal civic society and not an exclusively genealogical and vertical one. For example, it's our duty to think anew the relations between women and men outside of the family, in order to redefine civic relations between the two genders that would allow us to exit from the unculture of sexuality and the various forms of oppression and slavery that result from it.

R. BOFIGLIOLI: The answers provided by Freud and psychoanalysis to this kind of problem, as well as the traditional model of the "Left," have proven to be insufficient. They claim to be universals but they are actually founded and centered on one single subject: the masculine subject, and they've remained inside the patriarchal mythology. How can we go beyond these ideological dead-ends and create a different relationship to transcendence?

L. IRIGARAY: We've generally located transcendence between the "sky" and us. We should learn to lay it between us. Each one of us is inaccessible to the other, transcendent to him/her. The most irreducible space is between woman and man and it's only out of the impossibility of their reciprocal substitution — hence in the respect for each other's transcendence — that the social and cultural order can be thought anew and founded again. It is no longer acceptable that philosophy, politics, and religion be based on the model of the One, of the identical to oneself, which only tolerates a few hierarchized differences in relation to the One. Rather these diverse domains have to be rebuilt out of *two* different identities, where the transcendence of the (feminine) one in relation to the other becomes the place for the generation of words, creation, culture to happen. Unity then would no longer come from nature and resemblance but difference and the bridge, bridges, between things that are irreducible to the One. This new cultural foundation assumes that women who are not assimilated to a reproductive nature would receive an identity that would correspond to their sex and to their feminine gender.[14]

In this respect, it is obviously imperative to define a model for feminine identity. Certain women resist by invoking a traditional loss of identity on their part, based on an erroneous interpretation of democratic goals. Only an appropriate legislation could give women access to a real democracy. In the absence of such a legislation, a so-called democratic law of retribution often operates among women, which brings along with it a reduction of all women to the lowest human level. Each woman is annihilated in her identity because she has to remain one among others. This gesture, which has often been found among men in relation to an incult sexuality, is perpetuated by women themselves, probably as a result of a secular reduction to the status of "commodity," which turns them into rivals on the job market, on public representation, and in matters of love.

R. BOFIGLIOLI: Recognizing the existence of sexual difference in the figures of the divine and wondering what the feminine could be in terms of the divine (for example not holding onto the feminine divine as mother of son, but recognizing that it can exist between lovers, and in the genealogical relationship mother-daughter) implies that the woman be free in her gestures and in her words. This implies the reformulation of a new symbolic language, whether we have managed to achieve it or should still do so. What do you think about this?

L IRIGARAY: All our symbolic codes need to be reinterpreted as codes exclusively meant for the needs and desires of masculine subjects and for an economy of exchange among men. Fulfilling such a task requires time. However, in order to avoid a destruction dangerous for people and social communities, that is to say in order to avoid carelessly dilapidating our cultural heritage, I suggest starting again from an initial definition of the symbol: an object-sign divided in two to indicate a meeting between two people, linked to each other through this division, both out of faithfulness to themselves and to the entire object-sign.

I'm not saying that meaning has to remain inert; it can evolve, but still keeping in mind this initial obligation. Hence it would be possible to say that the origin of the symbolic is an alliance between two subjects and not an exchange of women between men. This being understood, the symbolic remains what it should be: a relationship of communication among people. Using the symbol in such a way is also a means of escaping the abstraction of a symbolic order which risks destroying the meaning and the subjects who obey its law.

R. BOFIGLIOLI: The latest literary and philosophical elaborations of women in the West lead to questioning freedom conceived as the free expression of oneself outside of any mediation. This would be the formulation or reformulation of a new symbolic universe that would respect the difference between the sexes. In your opinion, what are the new words, the new cultural and political means needed to achieve this formulation?

L. IRIGARAY: As I just said, I think the symbolic order has to be founded anew starting from the most simple gestures: sharing with the other — him or her — and being faithful to this sharing. Our culture being patriarchal, we have to remain alert to certain key points: refuse to accept a hierarchical relationship between men and women defined *a priori* and in a formal way; respect, in words and in acts, the natural and spiritual genealogy among women; reestablish a horizontal and vertical relation between men and women based on the respect of the two genealogies, in and for us, as well as for the other sex or the other gender; progressively organize a society of two sexes, two genders, both in cultural and political terms and in terms of the most intimate love. This means that political representatives will be men and women — male and female divinities, linguistic and cultural codes which are sexed in such a way that men and women will be represented in them with an equivalent value adequate to their difference in identity.

R. BOFIGLIOLI: For women who are trying to identify their difference, and attempting, as you write, "to get out of the negative which weighs upon them rather than endure it," Western culture has become for the most part something foreign. You talk about the necessity of restoring bridges between the Far-East, specifically the female aboriginal traditions of Hinduism, and Christianity. Can you elaborate on this subject?

L. IRIGARAY: Female aboriginal traditions respect nature and living places, the cult of local and personalized divinities, the concrete and mystical experience of religious phenomena. They are quite different from later Indo-European patriarchal tendencies which emphasize celestial divinities, speculations, and rites, especially magic ones.

The two traditions coexist in India and the practice of yoga can be found in both, with more aboriginal or patriarchal features. It seems to me that, in the New Testament, many features of Jesus' life belong to aboriginal female traditions:

1) There's an important relationship between nature and the spiritual: the birth of Jesus is announced by a star, his death is accompanied by cosmic phenomena and in his life intervene miracles linked to the economy of the universe.

2) Some of Jesus' attitudes are very close to those of yogis, in particular those who deal with the "miraculous" relationship to energy and breath.

3) Jesus' contradictory speeches recall the teachings of Buddha, and his "parables" are reminiscent of the poetic language of the monk in the most ancient traditions, especially India's.

4) The eucharist is a "vegetarian," non-sacrificial celebration of the fruits of the earth, which is reminiscent of female religious celebrations.

Obviously, the relationship between Jesus and his Father seems linked to the patriarchal cult of celestial divinities. But it's significant that only this aspect is commemorated and taught about Christ, whereas what in Jesus manifests his relationship to female traditions remains neglected, forgotten. In his teaching, Jesus suggests forgetting the diversity of traditions, or rather remembering them, but connecting them to each other. This point would explain how Jesus could also be called a "pontiff" between two worlds.

6

HISTORICAL PERSPECTIVES

CHIARA VALENTINI: How do you define your own approach as a philosopher in relation to other women's approaches to History?

LUCE IRIGARAY: It's easier, in a way, to place oneself outside of what's called History than outside philosophy. History is made up of characters, events, sequences of facts, that I can keep at a distance, look at, calculate. At least in our culture. Philosophy is concerned with the subject's birth and definition, namely in his relations to nature, language, the world, others. I realized that the subject of Western philosophy was male, not neutral or universal. No surprise there — throughout history, it's men who have written this philosophy. So, I had to critique their subject for not being singular and I had to try to define something that could be the woman-subject, as well as the relations this subject can have with itself and others: women and men. Of course, it's not easy to give oneself an *I,* but it's necessary to do so in order to become a *she.* Children start saying *I* before being able to imagine themselves as a *he* or *she.* In this way, women would have somehow learned to say *I* once in a while, but not "she" or "they"[15] [*elles*] yet. This is another stage in the becoming of the women's liberation that needs to be accomplished, so that women become adults and manage History along with men. In this co-management of humanity's present and future, by both women and men, the meaning of History will certainly change. This stage is difficult for women to carry out because, like children who hardly know how to say *I,* they find themselves facing a public, parental world made up of "they"[16] [*ils*], with no references to adult role-models that are women. Restricting them to the role of mothers forces them to remain infants, or a mere breeder without becoming *she*'s or *they*'s [*elles*].

C. VALENTINI: How do you justify your interest in religious traditions?

L. IRIGARAY: In this becoming "she," it's useful to build or rebuild a reference in our cultures, that of the *She,* of feminine transcendence. In more common language, let's say the reference to "God" or to the divinity for women. For centuries, we've been living under the reign of "He-God." This paralyzes the woman-becoming between either the Father-God's daughter or the Son-God's mother. Women are lacking a "She-God." I'm not for the simple reversal of values, in the sense of wishing that a reign of matriarchs would replace the patriarchs. I prefer the reign of lover couple-gods, divinized *he's* and *she's,* males and females, even in sexual love which is linked to the creation of the universe and other living beings. This has existed and still does in certain cultures, namely female aboriginal cultures. India, for example, still has traces of this type of culture. In India, women experience the best and the worst, in the sense that the most mysoginistic patriarchal traditions coexist with residual feminine aboriginal traditions. These traditions recognize the existence of lover couple-gods and women godesses, goddesses that are revered as women. Even the creator God — Vishnu — creates with his woman lover. In our tradition, the perspective is reversed: a single God creates the couple, and sexual love

64

isn't divinized. So, Jupiter, God of all gods, doesn't stick to only one lover, only to one marriage. In our culture, the masculine genealogical dimension monopolizes the divine dimension. Patriarchy has even erased the divinity of love between mothers and daughters, love whose traces we find in the couples Demeter-Kore and Anne-Mary, for example. In order to rediscover and improve in the culture of love between men and women, we need to restore the value of the mother-daughter relationship.

C. VALENTINI: Where is the place of women's cause in the unfolding of History?

L. IRIGARAY: We have to acknowledge that official History is partial and slanted. So, it often only involves half of humanity: the men. It privileges their values: their genealogy (father-son, natural or spiritual), war instincts, the desire to possess and capitalize in order to assert their power, contradictory urges between their need of a household with a woman-mother and their need to detach themselves from all that in order to make other conquests: other women, territories, possessions... Women who are recognized in History often share such values, even if they bring in some contrasts. So, these women win fame through their abilities as warriors, but for defending territories rather than invading them. Or even still: being faithful to a monotheistic religious tradition, they signal their lack of severity or fervor to the pontiffs. Their personality stands out, but they have a hard time imposing the singularity of their values. It's important to see how the role of women has been erased in relation to the role of men in the unfolding of History. Queens and goddesses progressively become subjugated. Women's worst fate in History is to (need to) claim their right to equality with men today.

C. VALENTINI: What is the origin of patriarchal power, in your opinion?

L. IRIGARAY: It's hard to define the exact origin of patriarchal power, all the more so since the traces leading up to this age in History have been erased and are still being erased today (including by burying archealogical traces underground). So, I'll give some possible motives for this cultural mutation, which has been happening progressively. I don't claim that the causes I enumerate are in strict chronological order:

• knowledge of man's role in procreating and subsequently founding a patriarchal kind of family;

• nomadism and, more specifically, the Aryan invasions which destroyed a large part of feminine aboriginal traditions;

• the passage from feminine civil and religious authority to the reign of the Father-God, of the Kings, their power and laws;

• the privilege of power, possession, war and sacrifice, over maintaining peace, justice, cohabitation and the respect and praise of natural fertility;

• the passage from a diet consisting of the earth's products: fruits, vegetables and cereals, to a carnivorous diet that necessitated hunting, and hence, force, violence and tools of war, in order to kill;

• the importance of alphabetical writing and logic, to a certain extent based on arbitrariness and the various beliefs that followed; etc.

C. VALENTINI: What are the most important discoveries that can be accredited to the women's liberation movements?

L. IRIGARAY: According to me, the re-discovery that neither the subect, language or God are neutral, that is to say without a sex or gender, and, consequently, we should rethink such values in the feminine so that a culture exists for women and also for the relations between women and men. Another re-discovery, linked to a practice that's become more common in women's lives again, is contraception: the possibility for them to cultivate their own nature, deciding whether or not to be a wife or, more importantly, to be a mother.

C. VALENTINI: Today, people often say "feminism is over." What do you think about this?

L. IRIGARAY: Saying feminism is over doesn't really mean much, unless we understand it as a stage that allowed women to become aware of their human identity. We should speak of a stage in History that's past, but not "over." Women's awareness, however, is far from being complete. So, feminism still serves a purpose. In some countries and branches of culture, it's really blossoming. Of course, there's a part of feminism that has its unpleasant excesses. But we have to be fair: up until now, feminism hasn't made weapons or mobilized armies. What's more, without feminism's excesses, neither contraception nor abortion, for example, would have become legal so quickly, in certain countries at least. I think feminism — I'd rather say: the followers of women's liberation, both men and women — today should be concerned with getting civil rights for women that suit their identity. There are two principal motives involved: not forcing women to slip into a man's skin or character in order to assume a public life (work, social relations), and not forcing women to personally defend themselves against rape, incest, involuntary prostitution and pornography, as well as all types of violence perpetrated against them — by turning to criminal law. Women still don't have these citizens' rights because they were considered minors, part of the father's or husband's familial possessions. They need to be recognized as full citizens, not only in terms of having possessions, but also in terms of people's respect and dignity. For women, existing as responsible citizens will lead to a new public representation, and also effective and free participation in managing society and History. This opens up the prospect of a real democracy in the future.

LOVING THE OTHER AS OTHER

Concerning *I Love to You* (*J'aime à toi*, 1992; Italian translation, 1993)

"The Civilization of the Two" (*Il Manifesto,* September 17, 1993); "Different From You/Different Between Us" (*Il Messagero,* June 1993); "The Question For Our Time" (*Taz,* 1992)

7

THE CIVILIZATION OF TWO

ROSSANA ROSSANDA: *Speculum* is the first theoretical response to the question: how does one establish a female identity in a conceptual universe where, until now, everything a single subject has thought, defined, and codified has been based on the other. How would you define *Speculum?*

LUCE IRIGARAY: I would say that *Speculum* is a book of philosophy that attempts to define the status of difference in contemporary reflection. The history of philosophy essentially unfolds as the history of thinking difference, differences. It is thanks to difference that thought is possible, and this must be examined in each era, so that it can be removed from opacity or simple empiricism.

In our anthropological age, starting with certain sciences called human sciences, the ultimate anthropological difference that requires examination is the one between man and woman. Philosophy's task is to raise this difference to a level of thought, to a somewhat ontological level; it's been left uncultivated, left to empiricism, and, in some ways, animality. This necessity becomes all the more imperative since a number of human liberation movements have brought men's exploitation of women into the open.

Certainly, ontology as well as traditional metaphysics find themselves radically modified by such thinking of difference, which confronts them with the task of recognizing the subject, consciousness, being as always being two, each irreducible to the other.

To approach the question of sexual difference is to realize that this difference has been forgotten, overlooked by the Western tradition. This has led to hierarchies and subordinations between One and the other, One and others, One and the multiple. Reintroducing the question of sexual difference today, therefore, makes one come up against speculative and practical resistances that are expressed, for example, by the refusal to consider women's alterity, different from that of an other among others, man being the patent or hidden model of the One.

R. ROSSANDA: I'm older than you. In school, college, politics, the secondarity or subalternity imposed upon women was clear to me, but it was as though it didn't concern me. It was held against me. The male construction of culture still fascinates me; it belongs to me and I belong to it. You, on the contrary, have always felt a resistance toward it. How did you consider it? An annoyance *vis-à-vis* your feminine experience or as a shortcoming of speculation itself?

L. IRIGARAY: I saw the problem as a personal resistance toward the theory of our tradition and as the internal shortcoming of its speculative construction. Our Western culture has not examined the relationship to nature and the body, to the macro- and microcosm seriously, as it seems both possible and beneficial to do; this has relegated thinkable realities to irrationality. Our tradition is equally lacking in terms of a philosophy of intersubjectivity. These limits exist in the development of other cultures, and even in the repression or censure exercised on some of them—in the Far East, for example. In our culture, the separation between philosophy and theology, philosophy and political practice, social practice, sexual practice is a problem, but so are the dichotomies between philosophy and science, philosophy and art. These dichotomies and hierarchies which go unquestioned by us are foreign to certain traditions. This is probably a good thing, and more appropriate to the way of thinking and practical modalities of female subjectivity. Often the cultures most favorable to the female gender are the ones that manifest these differences with our Western tradition.

R. ROSSANDA: The distinction between the rational and irrational is ancient. In the West, the irrational was not always defined in a negative way. It became negative when men defined affectivity, corporeity, perception as obscurity and attributed it to the feminine. Why accept that logos corresponds to the masculine and that the feminine remains outside logos, affirming as a value that which has been imposed on us as a limit?

L. IRIGARAY: It's a matter of questioning the foundations of Western rationality and asking yourself why a syllogism is thought to be more rational than the respect of nature, of the body, of the other, for example. In other words, why is our rationality historically based on abstract logical categories rather than on a culture of experience, including sensual experience? Such a culture, of course, exists in other traditions. For example, the culture of perception as such is very important in Far Eastern cultures, and it is accepted as, and is part of, the highest wisdom. It seems irrational to have forgotten these lessons and to hold on to an abstract rationality that stands in contrast to an immediate, still uncultivated, sensibility.

R. ROSSANDA: Has the lack of perception of sexual duality damaged the categories of language, the order and the very object of thought to the point of making them illegitimate for consciousness? Would you say: Hegel, I don't know; Freud, I don't know?

L. IRIGARAY: Certainly, we have to remember the existing tradition as an example of the mistakes that one shouldn't make again. We have to be aware of them to do better, not worse, to progress and not regress on the path of human civilization. We can question our tradition as well as the means that the male subject has given himself to escape his desire and anguish of a regression in nature: whether it's a matter of one's own mother, women, or of the natural world. Born of a woman with a body whose properties differ from the body of whoever engendered him, a man has to do a lot to construct his own identity; hence, a fair amount of slipping and irrationality in the construction of our Western mode of thinking. But perhaps the male subject himself could think differently in a tradition where sexual difference would be taken into account, and culture established by respecting the subjectivity both of the woman and that of the man, as other.

R. ROSSANDA: Each time a subject makes itself autonomous, it experiences what Gramsci calls a split phase: it separates itself and refuses the discourse that denied it. But this same discourse never exists in its entirety in the absence of the dominated subject: in the dominant discourse, there is an echo of the dominated, and vice versa. Women represent a gender and not a class; they are, for men, the occasion of an irreducible experience: of passion, doubt, confirmation or not of an identity. How does one account for this reality in the way we re-think ourselves?

L. IRIGARAY: If we are two different subjects, we must elaborate a culture that partially negates us as will or desire of being fully conscious of everything. To achieve a gendered subjectivity is to become the whole of oneself, with the condition of not being the whole of the subject, of consciousness, of being, etc. In this perspective, there is no longer a negation of the negation in the Hegelian sense but the constitution of another type of subject and culture.

As for Gramsci, it could be said that I am split between a subjectivity that wants to be absolute and an objectivity that is linked empirically to a history and, naturally or ontologically, to my belonging to a gendered body, and therefore to a gender. I do not produce the split through my thought: it already exists. I either recognize it or I don't.

The problem is that the subject, historically masculine, has a tendency to apprehend the negative as oppression, as external to oneself, and not enough as a process existing in itself/himself and necessary for the construction of an interiority. This path appears with the most coherence in the recognition of a double subjectivity: masculine and feminine. To grant equal dignity to two subjects is certainly not a worthless exercise, but it most often takes place within a world contructed in the masculine; it therefore implies a recognition "in the masculine" and the destruction of one of the two subjectivities. For this double subjectivity to exist, the masculine and feminine subjects and their relations have to be reshuffled differently. Getting to the bottom of things, as you like to say, rethinking man's being, woman's being and the private and collective constitution of intersubjectivity between the genders, can be accomplished by rethinking the values of our culture as monosexist, monogendered, falsely universal and partially imperialistic. Often emancipationists do not think in these terms, even if their actions are supposed to end in questions that are just as radical, if they are logical and honest. I think we're at a stage where this could happen.

R. ROSSANDA: In Italy, thinking of the feminine has developed in two directions. The first is self-awareness, the relationship between women, practice and word. This path emerged with the 1968 movement as anti-authoritarianism, unveiling new forms of oppression, and the modalities of introjected submission or secondary; it is often linked to psychoanalysis. Another direction claims to stem from your work, but, as far as I can tell, moves away from it; it emphasizes the exclusive relationship between women as a political foundation. How would you define your itinerary in relation to these two orientations?

L. IRIGARAY: I don't see the two currents as you describe them. The two currents that I am aware of are: one that emphasizes the conquest of equal rights and one—more radical and more theoreticized in an autonomous way as a women's liberation movement—demanding the right to difference. This current includes the stakes of autoconsciousness, women speaking out, the reflection and practice of a feminine genealogy, etc. These various tendencies of the movement that emphasizes difference are spread out over time, it's true: the reflection and practice of a feminine genealogy being a more recent kind of reflection among women. This pertains more to a cultural politics than to politics in the strict sense, as far as I am concerned, especially since — at least in the last few years, not in the first battles waged in the name of difference — it is often opposed to struggles directed towards positive rights, inherently political. As far as I'm concerned, I was involved in the various tendencies and periods of women's struggles. I was trained as a psychoanalyst and my work was often present in consciousness-raising groups. I respect the social tradition concerning equal rights even if I find it insufficient for human liberation, especially women's, and I theorized the necessity of respecting feminine genealogy in order to redefine a possible identity for a woman, for women, and for their relations. Still, I don't think this dimension suffices. To me, gender difference is conceived as difference with the other gender, as the difference between two genders, and not as a difference in relation to oneself, outside of the relationship with the other. Such a practice, in fact, risks overshadowing once again the importance of the boundary, the negative, which is necessary for conceiving and practicing difference, differences. I understand the strategy, but I consider it insufficient and problematic.

R. ROSSANDA: Your questioning "how" to communicate between the sexes, in *I Love to You*, starts with the thesis of the irreducibility of one sex to the other, the radical mistake of attempting to appropriate the other or to belong to the other. But isn't this just as true in a relationship between two people of the same sex? No one belongs to another person, because of each person's singularity, in body and mind, as an inviolable entity that one cannot possess without damaging oneself: certainly the woman, I admit, is physically and socially more easily wronged and injured. Moreover, doesn't the assertion of the unpossessability of the other, which I support, contradict the modalities of desire on the most basic level? Isn't this somehow rooted in the uncertainty of the "I," the need to return to the maternal body? Isn't there a "tragic" opposition, in the literal sense, between relation and desire? Or is female desire of a different nature, does it obey another functioning?

L. IRIGARAY: Of course, each person is different. But this infinite differentiation of individuals does not allow one to structure relationships in twos or collectively. It remains on the horizon of the opposition between the One and the multiple. The indefinite differences between individuals indefinitely destructure the community that must find a unifying principle in order to organize itself. The apparent tolerance concerning the indefinitely different may lead to blind support of various forms of totalizing powers. To think in terms of difference between men and women at once means pursuing the constitution of human identity, the construction of History and giving oneself a way of defining a non-totalizing-totalitarianizing principle of communal organization. This principle attempts, moreover, to establish new bridges between nature and culture, between instincts or drives and civility, between the individual body and the collective body. Such a course is necessary in order to account for the cultural lessons of the last few years and offset the diverse, more or less explicit, forms of sexism, racism, fascism.

R. ROSSANDA: In *I Love to You* you write that a threshold of silence, of refraining from appropriating, is a necessary condition for the two genders to communicate. And you propose that women do their part without demanding awareness and reparation from the other sex. Some object that, as long as the male subject has not at least attempted to take two steps giving up dominating and giving up considering himself as the universal, there is the fear that your proposal would lead back to non-conflictual relations that won't help the development of feminine autonomy. How do you respond to that fear?

L. IRIGARAY: The necessity of silence, of what is impossible to say in relation to the other gender, signifies above all the respect of a limit in terms of what can be said of one of the two genders. This is a way of making sure that each gender will not have the right to speak for the other, to speak in their place, to impose norms thought to be adapted to these necessities, etc. To wait for the other to act first is not to assume one's share of the negative. Now, to take this upon oneself, especially as a woman, can change the relationship between the genders, whereas putting the other on trial can only maintain hierarchical and alienating relations. I do not think that making the work of the negative enter the relations between women and men, whether in a couple or a community, whether private or civil (I only use this opposition only to make myself understood), implies a regression in the establishment of a culture of two genders. This represents the possibility of a new era of History as a civilization with, and between, two subjects.

R. ROSSANDA: There is a great temptation in relations between women trying to think in terms of the feminine. It seems that models of liberation are almost always reproduced in the masculine: each woman feels oppressed, intolerance is high, women all emphasize the divisions. Why this obsessive repetition in the conquest of subjectivity? Why do you speak so little among yourselves? Why is there so much bitter distrust, so much fear of being polluted by the other? Why don't women seek a different mode of being?

L. IRIGARAY: It's hard. Going from nature to culture is not easy, nor is emerging from slavery. Women suffer and cause others to suffer for this birth. Sometimes, it's necessary to take a rest, to not accept to immolate yourself, to refuse to do harm as well, as this other world comes into being. Staying alive seems to me to be a part of liberation, of one's liberation, for a woman, and also of respecting another's life. This sometimes requires a bit of a retreat, stepping back a little, continuing the work differently, elsewhere. Personally, for years, I've been pursuing it with women in my neighborhood, working-class women, women from the country, shopkeepers, as much as with intellectuals. I've spoken to so many women, and listened to so many women since 1970, especially 1974, you can't imagine! It shows in my books on some level, but the individual and even collective publications [the articles and even the anthologies] that I have managed to do up until now, are far from representative of all the dialogues I've had with women of diverse social, cultural, and political backgrounds. Your objection concerning non-communication among women does not seem to me to concern women who are really involved with the liberation of women, for whom greeting, hospitality, communication, have always been the primary means of practicing a politics of liberation. Certainly, once again, there are cases where this is difficult: due to fatigue, a block, a lack of intermediary, a lack of clarity. I don't think it's a simple refusal to communicate.

Translated by Jeanine Herman

8

Different From You / Different Between Us

FIORELLA IANNUCCI: What does the title *I Love to You* mean?

LUCE IRIGARAY: "I Love to You" means: I don't take you as an object of my love or desire. I love you as irreducibly other. I keep a "to" as an inalienable space between us, a guarantor of your freedom and mine. "I love to you" means that I maintain a relationship of in-direction with you in order to avoid any amorous possession or consumption and, by doing this, I protect the two that we are and the relationship between this two: I love *to* you like I talk *to* you. "I love to you" is a way to respect your intention and mine, and also a way to make the "between us" last. "I love to you" means that I will never entirely know you and that to love you implies respecting the mystery that you will always be for me. "I love to you" means many other things too which can be found in the book, and also things for each one of us (male and female) to discover on our own.

F. IANNUCCI: Why did you dedicate *I Love to You* to a man? Who is this man?

L. IRIGARAY: In the "Prologue," I explain why I dedicated this book to Renzo Imbeni. I also mention this dedication, more poetically, on the back of the French book jacket. It's hard to summarize in a few words the intention behind this dedication. I can only place Renzo Imbeni. When I met him for the first time, he was the mayor of Bologne, and I was invited to be a debate partner with him when he was elected to the European Parliament. His behavior during the debate touched me; he was rigourous, audacious and respectful all at once. Renzo Imbeni knows how to listen to the other, recognize his/her worth, and publicly assert it. Nevertheless, he remains faithful to himself. Hence it's possible to be and remain two with him: a woman and a man in a political and civic relationship, who don't relinquish their sensitive qualities or their sexual difference. This may seem banal; but, actually, it's very rare. Aside from the friendship he inspired in me, I wanted to work with him politically. We did a study together on European citizenship in the framework of the European Parliament; it's in the book *The Civilization of the Two*.

F. IANNUCCI: You're politically active with him. But this isn't the first time you've been in politics. What's changed in your relationship to politics?

L. IRIGARAY: We *practice* the difference between man and woman and try to impart that a civic relationship respectful of this difference can serve as a general model for democracy. We try to put our sexual, cultural and political differences into use towards defining a new politics: more fair, more fruitful, happier. This kind of politics is above all founded on relationships between male and female citizens — firstly between a male citizen and a female citizen — whose identities are secured by laws for real people, that is to say laws for men and women. I have believed for a long time that women should unite to obtain rights of their own. This goal was shared by 70s activists, thanks to whom new laws for women were made, including the right to have an abortion. In my opinion, defining special laws for women is still one of the primary duties of a democratic government. But not all of today's "feminists" share this point of view. They often fear the law as something that could subject them to the State, without understanding that civil rights specific to the persons actually represent a possibility for male and female citizens to maintain an autonomy and a tension in relation to State institutions. Too many women forget that for a subjective growth, especially one that's collective, mediations are necessary, including judicial mediations.

F. IANNUCCI: Why combine politics and love like you do?

L. IRIGARAY: According to me, all politics should strive to make love reign between citizens. When political life is dependent on the power of a leader, of his government and of State organizations, even democratic election isn't enough to ensure citizens' peaceful and civil coexistence. A cohabitation based on property is a source of wars, not an insurance of convivial living. It's sort of the same thing with a society that claims to be egalitarian, but where the non-acknowledgment of differences only generates conflicts. The primary goal of politics should be ensuring peace, harmony and happiness among the citizens. This can't happen unless a society's main priorities are the rights of each person in his/her uniqueness, as well as in his/her desire for a respectful relationship with the other. Hence my suggestion to rebuild democracy on an infinite number of relationships between women and men which respect their differences. This allows for a truly democratic, living civil community to be built. Respecting sexual difference encourages the respect of other differences.

F. IANNUCCI: You stress the difference between men and women. But aren't relationships between daughter and mother, and between women in general, also made up of differences?

L. IRIGARAY: The difference between mother and daughter is primarily in the genealogical dimension. The relationship of transcendence between them is in some way vertical, or at least would be vertical if the mother really remained a woman and didn't reduce herself to the natural function of engendering. Differences between women in the horizontal dimension are more existential. They're linked to different stories but not to a different relationship with being or identity. These differences are often manifested quantitatively and competitively even when they're qualitative: she's more beautiful than I am, she's more intelligent than I, etc.... The difference between man and woman is a difference in being, a difference between two worlds, which resists any quantitative assessment. Man and woman are irreducible one to the other, and the difference between them cannot be evaluated, calculated and appropriated. It always remains insurmountable, like the mystery that some blindly call "God." "God" ought to be located elsewhere or beyond this horizontal transcendence between man and woman. The divine also ought to be spoken in two genders or bisexually in one sole being and not only in the masculine.

F. IANNUCCI: You suggest moving from a culture of need placed in the neutral to a culture of communication between us. Can you elaborate on this idea?

L. IRIGARAY: Actually, our cultural tradition most often still holds onto needs: the need to eat, materially and spiritually, but also the need to be sheltered, to be clothed, to gain some knowledge and information, and even to possess. So, communication is subordinate to needs. Our culture has hardly developed inter-communication or inter-subjectivity, very much, and as a result we aren't aware that subjects are different. Subjects are reduced to the same needs or to the status of owners, among whom differences are quantitative and not qualitative. In this case, communication is placed in the neuter and remains there because it's more mindful of the object than the subjects, and it's unaware of the difference between the subjects. Communication also works like this in transferring information. It hasn't yet reached the point of an inter-subjective exchange.

F. IANNUCCI: So then, are you saying that sexual difference would be a necessary condition for us to communicate with each other? And that to get to this point, we have to be faithful to our feminine identity or to our gender, for fear of committing an ethical mistake?

L. IRIGARAY: In sexual difference, the fact that men and women belong to two different worlds forces them to communicate between them in order to overcome their instinctual silence or submission to the undifferentiation of need. So, it's a question of addressing someone other than yourself in order to have an inter-subjective exchange with him/her: an exchange of words, not an exchange of objects. The challenge in communication here is to really dialogue and not just transmit information. This dialogical relation between man and woman, men and women remains to be invented, almost entirely from scratch. It represents an important stage in human civilization that has yet to be accomplished. It requires man and woman to be faithful to their gender and to start communicating from their differences, and not get rid of them.

F. IANNUCCI: So, for you, sexual difference implies a relationship with the other gender, and not simply saying "I am different"?

L. IRIGARAY: Yes. "I am different" can just be a stage meant to end subjugation to the other gender. This stage ought to ensure objective mediations of language, of representations, of specific rights, and not remain a simple subjective demand. These kinds of objective mediations help in both the development of the feminine subject and its possible representation for the other gender. Just saying "I am different from" is another way of taking male subjectivity as a yardstick: I am different *from* you, *from* your history. There is still no recognition of difference as a place for a relationship with the other gender: we are different, one from the other. It's true that, in such a case, the yardstick is unlimited. It is difference itself that insures the relationship. But difference isn't something that can be grasped...

F. IANNUCCI: How can we use language in our relation to the other gender and to our own kin, in order to avoid all forms of submission, fusion and lack of differentiation ?

L. IRIGARAY: At first, women learned to say *I*. They still very rarely talk about, and to, *she(s)*. And they represent and speak of themselves even less as *I-she*. The surveys I do with other researchers — both men and women — concerning the way men and women speak show that this tendency exists in different languages and cultures. So, it's a matter of interpreting the answers not only in terms of personal pronoun usage but in terms of the totality of representations through which the subject refers to him/herself and the other, the others. I think learning to say *I-she* is an important stage in avoiding fusion and submission. Asserting oneself only as *I* is both too subjective and too abstract, too undif-ferenciated. Saying *I-she* is a way for women to auto-repre-sent themselves on their own, assert their belonging to a gender, to a concrete objectivity that protects against fusion and undifferentiation. It's also a requisite linguistic victory to find out how to communicate between *I-she(s)* and also to discover the path of possible dialogues with *you-he(s)* with-out renouncing oneself or nullifying the other as other.

F. IANNUCCI: Do you have an idea or a wish concerning the future of woman/women's liberation?

L. IRIGARAY: In my opinion, the major stages that need to be accomplished at this time are:

1. Securing rights that give women a civil identity and not only a natural one;

2. A culture of sexuality and affectivity that allows per-ceptible social victories not to be nullified in love relation-ships or in the intimacy of the home or the family;

3. Reciprocal recognition between man and woman, men and women, that implies using a negative that's open to the existence of two genders, two subjects. Of course, all these stages require developing languages appropriate to each one of the two genders, as well as developing a lan-guage that allows for exchanges between them.

9

THE QUESTION FOR OUR TIME

ELKE WEBER: If every age had one question to think about, what would this question be in our time?

LUCE IRIGARAY: Every age has one major question to address. I'm neither the only one nor the first one to say it. For example, Heidegger, and Hegel in his own way, have already said it. What I mean is that at the basis of many theoretical and practical issues and opening a passage from the past to the future, a question could be found that solves urgent necessities and allows for a development of civilization. This question embodies both a philosophical interrogation and political imperatives. Sexual difference, in our time, seems to be at the intersection of all these dimensions. It's being raised after Freud and his discovery of the unconscious and the libido, after Marx and his analyses of socio-economic injustices, after the deconstruction of the subject by the last Western philosophers, after the sexual liberation and women's liberation movements... This question regroups many civic and religious sectors. It seems to allow for a becoming of the human element to grow and also for a more fair and democratic, potentially inter-cultural and inter-religious theory and practice of the universal to be established.

E. WEBER: In your new book *I Love to You,* you write that "our interpretation of human identity was theoretically and practically incorrect." As far as theory goes, where's the flaw in our interpretation?

L. IRIGARAY: In thinking that the subject is *one*, that the mark of gender is secondary, that language, no matter how it's marked by the sexed dimension, could be an instrument for the discovery of a universal truth; in thinking that expressing or representing the majority of our values by the masculine gender was a normal situation…

E. WEBER: Who is the *we* of *our* interpretation?

L. IRIGARAY: The Western culture to which we belong.

E. WEBER: How could we find a more correct interpretation of our human identity?

L. IRIGARAY: By defining a human identity that would be more consistent with the real, hence double. We are men and women, irreducible to each other. We are *two human genders*, not just one. We must not confuse gender and species.

E. WEBER: *I Love to You* is a strange expression. Why didn't you choose "I love you" as the title for your book?

L. IRIGARAY: *I Love to You* suggests the necessity for a relationship that's indirect, intransitive meant to maintain the *two* in the relationship between the genders. "I love you" always runs the risk of reducing the other to the *object* of my love. We are no longer *two* to love each other in an intersubjective relationship. The *to* is the place where the intention of the one and the other can meet. I love to what you are, to what you want, to what your intention is. I renounce possessing and having you, in order to be and build something with you.

E. WEBER: In *I Love to You* you focus on heterosexual relationships in search of sexual identity. Why couldn't women or men define their sexual identity with someone of the same sex?

L. IRIGARAY: We are begotten by woman and man, we live in a society of women and men. Whatever our sexual choice may be, we have to resolve the question of the two human genders' cohabitation, in and with each other. Anyhow, in *I Love to You* I spell out how the relationship between woman/women and man/men can become non-hierarchical, non-instinctual. The book's objective is to create a culture of the relationship between genders. But this culture can become a model for a relationship in their diversity.

E. WEBER: If the subjectivity of women and men is different, will an intersubjectivity between the sexes be possible?

L. IRIGARAY: The difference between woman and man allows for an intersubjectivity that wouldn't subject the one and the other to nature, to the same, to the equal, to imperatives, to laws, to their external realities. This requires that the one and the other recognize their own limits in that they belong to only one gender. To be a woman means not to be a man and to be a man means not to be a woman. This *not* becomes an instrument and a place for each person's identity and a creative, and not only procreative, intentional relationship between the two to be established. Being able to identify with the other seems to me an ambiguous cultural improvement. Learning to cohabitate and live with the other in intercultural relationships, in a couple as well as in a larger civic community, represents the most necessary progress since sexual difference is the fundamental paradigm of the difference between us. To forget this is running the risk that other differences would exacerbate.

E. WEBER: And how will we say *we/us* between man/men and woman/women?

L. IRIGARAY: The *we/us* between the genders would then be a cultivated, civilized *we/us*, owing to a respect for the *not*. It's not gregarious, undifferentiated, or simply positive. It's always spiritual and at the same time tangible.

E. WEBER: Why did you dedicate *I Love to You* to Renzo Imbeni, an Italian politician?

L. IRIGARAY: Because "I love to him," in his way of being personal and political. Because he is the only politician who has publicly recognized my work, especially in a debate with him where my position, his position, and especially his electors' position, were different. Because it's possible to be *two* with him — a man and a woman — in a relationship of civility. Because speaking with him is possible, without one being subjected to the other. Because at least part of our intentions, his and mine, we can share. Because he's a member of the European Parliament.

E. WEBER: What is typically feminine in your philosophy?

L. IRIGARAY: Criticizing the patriarchy and the phallocracy elaborated from a place that's outside their empire, defining mediations I feel are necessary for establishing a feminine identity, and a taste for intersubjectivity, especially with the other gender. And also: the real, and not abstract, concern for life, future life on this earth, the act of giving breath to whoever reads me without forcing them to be locked into a system. And probably the way of thinking and writing, the logic and the style.

EQUALITY AND/OR DIFFERENCE?

Concerning *Thinking the Difference* (*Penser la différence, 1989*)

From: "The Time of Difference" (*Famille rurales,* September 1995)

10

THE TIME OF DIFFERENCE

PATRICK DE SAGAZAN: Can we truly say that women and men are different in spite of sharing the same human nature?

LUCE IRIGARAY: The word "nature" is a quite recent, abstract and ambiguous term because it has so many meanings. It doesn't exist for the Greeks, for whom it would rather correspond to: "coming to appear" — to be born in a certain sense — growing... terms which are far more concrete. "Human nature" is seen more in opposition to other natures, "divine nature" for example, than to account for our identity as man and as woman.

Maybe it would be better to talk about the human species as being divided into two genders, using a word that means "genus," "generation" or "family" among the Greeks, and leave the word "nature" for more speculative, philosophical or theological considerations. For lack of words, it would be better to maintain that human nature is *two:* each gender having its own characteristics that are irreducible to *one* nature.

P. DE SAGAZAN: How are men and women different?

L. IRIGARAY: Men and women are corporeally different. This biological difference leads to others: in constructing subjectivity, in connecting to the world, in relating.

I'll explain: the little girl is born a woman of another woman, with the capacity to bring others into the world. She will have a relationship with her mother and to generation that is different from the little boy's. From the very beginning, the little girl finds herself in a relationship of identity and familiarity with the woman who conceived her. The relationship between two subjects is therefore easier for her than for the boy, who has to build it with his mother in terms of difference, using objects, identification with the father, etc....

Another example: woman engenders *in herself*, makes love *in herself*. Man engenders and makes love *outside of himself*. This means that their relationship to themselves and their relationship to the other are far from being similar, favoring either the inside *or* the outside, either refuge in oneself *or* respect for the other outside of oneself.

Another characteristic distinguishing men and women: a woman has the capacity to feed from her body, a man feeds more from his work.

From conditions such as these, girls and boys, women and men have to acquire both a unity and a world of their own that are necessarily different. And it is right that for every woman and man, and for their way of relating, that things are like this.

P. DE SAGAZAN: Does woman operate differently than man in the spheres of intellect, will, and feeling, in her way of existing in the world?

L. IRIGARAY: From birth, men and women belong to different worlds, biologically and relationally, which they'll cultivate in their own ways if they stay faithful to their gender and avoid assuming a neutral identity. One characteristic of this difference is that the female world remains closer to what's naturally preordained, meshing herself with it in her own becoming, whereas the male world is built, in part against nature. That doesn't mean that woman's subjectivity is reduced to being pure nature and man's, culture. Rather, the two genders have different forms of consciousness: one remaining more faithful to the body and to her sensibility, to the concrete environment, and to intersubjective relationships, particularly in terms of two; the other, constructing a universe of non-natural objects, through a specific technique which also translates into forming human groups generally far more removed from natural elements than those organized by women.

P. DE SAGAZAN: What is the importance of sexuality in the constitution of a person?

L. IRIGARAY: Sexuality can be understood in two ways. First, as anything concerning the sexual act and reproduction. Even when reduced to that, it's still significant since it deals with life and love. But the words "sexual" or "sexed" take on a much broader meaning when we put them together with other words. Thus "sexed identity" designates the global identity of the individual, man or woman, and the expression "sexual energy" can signify the whole array of drives, desires or attractions that animate us, whether they are strictly expressed on the sexual level or are displaced into various activities. These activities can remain instinctive, such as the appetite, but they can also be exercised on the cultural level, becoming artistic creation for example.

P. DE SAGAZAN: What is the specific contribution of women in every human society?

L. IRIGARAY: I would say: a relational quality that is more respectful of life and people, a larger concern for the immediate environment, especially the natural environment. But I'm not familiar with every human society…

P. DE SAGAZAN: What would women's contribution be if our technological and market-oriented societies were to breathe with their two lungs?

L. IRIGARAY: Women could develop a culture of life and love, something that we often relegate to the beyond because we don't know how to practice it here below. They could bring a respect between us of singularity and differences, especially in terms of sex, as well as the taste for joy in one's relationship to nature and to the other.

P. DE SAGAZAN: What symbolic representations of woman are there in Western language and gesture?

L. IRIGARAY: Western culture has generally defined the woman's role as faithful spouse and housewife — mother, socially and civilly submissive to the man-father-citizen. At the same time, it has exalted the sexual function of the woman-whore, arousing male desire using her charms, her garments, and stupidity. None of these representations are adequate. They don't take into account the singularity and dignity of the woman as person.

P. DE SAGAZAN: Where does freedom fit into a reformulation of men-women relations?

L. IRIGARAY: The redefiniton of gender identities can open up a new stage for the becoming human. There are still traces of instincts derived from animality and human passions in the relations between women and men: for instance, the instinct to possess the other's body like a property. Some can go beyond themselves towards a fuller freedom where "sexed belonging" becomes a dimension of consciousness and not just a natural given. Respect of the other gender, the most difficult kind of respect since it leads from the most instinctive to the most spiritual, can bring us to respect other differences: race, generation, tradition, language, and culture.

In our age especially, each person must learn to be faithful to him/herself in the acknowledgement and love of the other, the others. Sexual difference, a universal difference, can serve as a base for this learning experience.

A CULTURE AND A
POLITICS OF TWO
SUBJECTS

Concerning *To Be Two* (*Essere Due,* first published in
Italian, 1994)

From: "Man-Woman in Search of Harmony" (*La Gazzetta del Sud,* April 5, 1994); "Different but United Through a New Alliance" (*Il Messagero,* April 11, 1994); "Luce, The Teaching of Difference" (*L'Arena,* April 29, 1994)

11

MAN AND WOMAN IN SEARCH OF HARMONY

MARIA ANGELA MASINO: What is the political objective of a culture of sexual difference?

LUCE IRIGARAY: Trying to conceive and practice a new relationship between woman and man, women and men, undoubtedly is related to a search for harmony both in private and public life. I can give two reasons. First, it presupposes cultivating urges, instincts and affects in order to learn to respect the other while respecting oneself. This implies a culture of immediate feelings, of "natural" attraction. Our Western tradition is still lacking this culture, to such an extent that physical love often seems to be something almost animal, instinctual, that's "made up for" by the fact that it produces children. Physical love also seems to be a sort of fatality that can't be governed or managed, in which man is the active, dominating pole, and woman is the passive pole, the extremity that experiences pleasure, which arouses the man. So, a culture of love and attraction between man and woman — like the one I try to define — is certainly heading towards a greater search for harmony. Because this culture presupposes respecting the difference between the sexes and genders, however, it's also a way to learn how to respect other differences we're faced with: differences between cultures, races, ages, religions, etc. On another level, it represents a pathway to cohabitation, a coexistence of all men and women in harmony.

M. A. MASINO: What is the meaning of the word "liberty" in the context of human liberation and, more specifically, in the context of women's liberation?

L. IRIGARAY: In our Western history and even today, we often take becoming free for liberating ourselves from external constraints: from an employer for example, or from a culture or nation that has invaded us and imposed laws on us, or even more recently for women, liberating themselves from masculine power. It seems to me that becoming free presupposes just as much, if not more, a personal effort which doesn't simply mean liberating ourselves from something or someone external to us but also liberating ourselves from habits, inertias which we find inside ourselves. So, for the woman, in love or in a couple, to assume that she occupies the passive pole, the pole that experiences love or pleasure, and not the one that can actively love — not only the child but also the man — and to consider herself the one who can bring desire to the other and not just the desire for me as woman through seduction but desire for more fulfillment of her identity, personality, etc. This way of becoming free, then, corresponds to a new task that everyone needs to accomplish, especially women. I don't believe that only a change on men's part is going to make us women more free, building a personal interiority is also or primarily a change in relation to ourselves, to our becoming, our way of being. Being and remaining two in the couple, in all forms of couples, in all meetings between men and women, corresponds to achieving a liberty that's not merely won against aggressivity or conflict towards the other sex or gender, but achieving one's own identity as well as the ability to be faithful to oneself. This is difficult for women but it's really worth the effort and it's a prerequisite for being able to live and love in reciprocity.

M. A. MASINO: Is it possible to remain two in love and desire?

L. IRIGARAY: Yes, it's possible in trying to discover the other as other: an other that I will never be and never know, that remains inaccessible and transcendent to me. I think that recognizing the other's alterity requires more emphasis on perception than on sensation. If I simply experience joy or sorrow, desire or disgust, because of the other we are no longer really two. I lose the other in the sensation, in the feeling I experience. In a way, I consume him in order to feel him, and this way of reducing the other to feelings is a more feminine way of reducing the other to oneself and, in a way, possessing him. Whereas if I perceive the other as other, I always leave him outside of me, even if I feel him inside myself. In this way, I let him have his autonomy and his freedom and I make it possible for my meeting with him to always be an adventure, a new discovery: what I perceive of him is something different each time we meet. Of course, this difference corresponds to a sensorial perception: my eyes, my ears, my nose, my touch, but, if I respect the other as other, an intimate perception develops in me which allows me to internalize the other while respecting him as different and external to me. So it's possible to remain two and learn how to be together while remaining one and the other, without possessing, without merging and without consuming.

M. A. MASINO: Could you tell us how to maintain the two by giving some examples?

L. IRIGARAY: I'll use the example of the title *I Love to You* to explain what I mean. The intentional agrammaticality of this title warns against saying "I love you," which always runs the risk of reducing the other to the object of my love.

Often it happens like this: the subject-man loves the woman who becomes his object in love, the subject-mother loves the child who becomes her object in love. In this case, there's never really love because love implies two subjects who love each other. The indirection of "to you" is a way of handling the existence of two subjects and a space between them which maintains their irreducibility to each other. Saying "I love to you" is bringing love to a way of speaking between us: to love to, like saying to talk to. In the book *To Be Two*, there's a long passage about the caress in the first chapter: "The Wedding of Body and Words." In this passage I try to show how the caress can become a reciprocal word-touch between people who love each other and not a capture by the hand or the gaze as it's often described by male philosophers like Jean-Paul Sartre, Maurice Merleau-Ponty and Emmanuel Levinas.

M. A. MASINO: In *I Love to You* and *To Be Two*, you give quite a bit of attention to silence. Why?

L. IRIGARAY: In *I Love to You* and *To Be Two* I talked about silence as a condition of love between men and women. Silence is a way of respecting and acknowledging the fact that there's a difference between man and woman. Of course, this difference requires us to speak in order to communicate, but words can come only after a time of silence, a pause that takes care of the space that lies in the insurmountable difference between man and woman. This silence between them is also a way of questioning the power of any knowledge derived from the genealogical relationship: the father, and sometimes the mother, often claim to know everything about the child. The silence between genders or sexes is a way of coming out of the power and the dependence that exist in both natural and spiritual genealogies. I also mentioned begetting silence between man and woman in *To Be Two*. I talked about silence the way one conceives of the child when we say that the child is *one,* and this one doesn't preserve the difference between man and woman. I tried to show how in order to keep loving each other man and woman have to beget silence, a condition of their becoming, each on one's own and together. Merely begetting children would be a way of forgetting the lovers' sexed dimension in order to be exclusively parents, somewhat neglecting the respect and love between them. Aside from the need for silence, I showed other ways of getting to know and cultivating the difference between men and women, strategies that allow for both of them not to give themselves up and abandon their own initiatives in love: indirection, the culture of perception, touching the other while respecting him and myself as being different, that is to say, without destroying subjectivity in the touch — creation between man and woman as a way to overcome belonging to a natural genealogy, a genealogy and an attraction that would only be natural, etc.

M. A. MASINO: You talk about the danger of the master-slave relationship between women and men. Do you think this relationship can exist between women? For example, between mother and daughter?

L. IRIGARAY: Obviously the master-slave relationship can exist between mother(s) and daughter(s). Many aspects make it possible: the mother's authority over the daughter; the fact that the mother often claims to know more than the daughter, so the daughter has to obey her; the daughter's duty to respect and confide in the mother; the acknowledgment of genealogical power; the relationship with death that somehow puts the mother-daughter poles on the same footing with the master-slave poles. Of course, one would have to carefully elaborate on the differences involved in this master-slave relationship, whether in terms of nature or knowledge or even work. But remaining or going back to a mother-daughter relationship certainly won't be enough to escape from the master-slave relationship.

M. A. MASINO: Could you signal some key words for readers embarking on *I Love to You* and *To Be Two*?

L. IRIGARAY: I can suggest some words that evoke what's introduced and elaborated in *I Love to You*. First, the word "intersubjectivity." A large part of the history of philosophy, and even Western politics, always refers to a solitary subject or a subject who lives communally with other similar subjects; it doesn't really address the relationship between two subjects inasmuch as they're different. The relationship between man and woman provides a decisive position from which to conceive and practice their relationship between two different subjects. The intersubjective relationship in sexual difference can allow for the realization of intersubjectivity on both the private and the civic and political levels.

Another word for reading *I Love to You* and *To Be Two* is "horizontality." In both books, I try to establish a human relationship that wouldn't be solely determined by the verticality of genealogy. I think that a horizontal relationship between man and woman means attaining human maturity, coming out of infantile dependence on the natural, spiritual or political father or mother. The model of horizontality has yet to be conceived in our culture and it assumes that man is no longer woman's master and that woman is no longer the all powerful mother of the child, or indeed of the husband.

Practicing horizontality between men and women demands that they reach a relationship of "creation" between them. This creative work enables the relationship between man and woman to exit a relationship that's solely natural while respecting their natural belonging as sexual beings. Practicing horizontality also introduces into the relationship between the sexes a cultural task that needs to be fulfilled, whether it's on the level of the couple, the family or the civil community. In this way, the relationship between man and woman becomes a community value, a political value, a value of civilization.

Another important word that crops up in both books, perhaps more explicitly in *I Love to You*, is the word "listening." Listening to the other as an other is a way of bringing the natural attraction between men and women to the dimension of words, of dialogue and of exchange between them. Listening to the other is repeating him/her as such and simultaneously creating a place for exchange between them. Listening to the other is a way of coming out of possession, fusion and submission or domination.

M. A. MASINO: How can we reach this relationship of two (*à deux*) that you suggest, especially between genders, if we are all interdependent, especially financially?

L. IRIGARAY: First, we need to question the fact that our interdependence is solely defined in relation to money. If we accept that money is what determines it, we've already made money our absolute master. The power of money is a problem that played a part in a configuration which already included other relationships of dependence, or determined other relationships of dependence. I'm obviously thinking about patriarchal culture which, for the most part, is accompanied by a culture that emphasizes possessing goods. By emphasizing ownership, the patriarchy brought along with it women's and children's dependence on the patriarch. Now,

with the power of money today, women and children are still
dependent. So, it's not possible to merely talk about interdependence between men and women. Women need to attain
subjective autonomy in order for a real interdependence to
exist. In my opinion, the objective of woman's subjective
autonomy or independence doesn't have to be separation
from the male world; rather, the objective should be finding
a way to establish a new relationship of both respect and
interdependence between the sexes or genders in private
life, as well as in civil and political life.

M. A. MASINO: How do you see the role of "parity" in liberation struggles led by women?

L. IRIGARAY: To a certain degree, struggles for parity are
legitimate emancipatory battles. But it's important that they
don't just remain a strategy for women's liberation and more
generally for the liberation of the human genders. Actually,
if parity seems to be the ultimate goal, then there's the risk
of confusing the right to a certain equivalence of social roles
with women achieving the right to be equal to men. The risk
is twofold: from a social standpoint, women's liberation is
presented as a right to attain a world that's actually male; a
right to masculine, not feminine, values; in other words, a
right to become full-fledged men and not a right to assert a
female identity on all levels. Very often, the right to parity
doesn't take into consideration the different values that suit
men, on the one hand, and women on the other; so, there's
the risk of its bringing along with it an identity loss for
women, a neutralization of the identity linked to gender.
What seemed to be liberation then turns in on itself and
becomes its opposite.

Parity is also generally conceived from social values
and attaining a human identity can't be reduced to attaining

social values, a human identity also implies building one's own interiority. Let me give an example: women, and also men, who have cared about parity most, have generally not thought too much about the difference in words, images and representations corresponding to a man's identity on the one hand and a woman's on the other. Even so, these are obviously deciding factors, as much on the man's side as on the woman's, in the discovery and assertion and involvement on both sides of a subjectivity.

12

DIFFERENT BUT UNITED
THROUGH A NEW ALLIANCE

FIORELLA IANNUCCI: Why did you first write *To Be Two* in Italian?

LUCE IRIGARAY: I had wanted to write in Italian for several years. Italian is close to me, I find it beautiful and I love it. Maybe because it's part of my genealogy: my father's mother was Italian. My desire to write in Italian became more intense when *I Love to You* was translated into Italian: it was difficult for me to accept that someone other than myself would express the words I wrote in *I Love to You*, and all the more so that the book is dedicated to an Italian man, who is very much alive and to whom I speak in Italian. *To Be Two* is the continuation of *I Love to You*, and I wanted to write this book in Italian myself. Besides, I have conversations with a lot of Italian women and men and it's become artificial to put a translator of either sex between us. For me, Italian is a language of beauty and love; it's most certainly out of love that I wanted to write *To Be Two* in Italian.

F. IANNUCCI: If men and women are different, how can they communicate?

L. IRIGARAY: I'm often asked this question: if men and women are different, how can they enter into a relationship?

To ask this is to forget that desire exists between them. It seems that desire is often born of difference, especially between man and woman, but also through other differences. On the other hand, the economy of exchanges between us hasn't yet succeeded in translating difference(s) in terms of communication between speakers. This economy has often been reduced to communicating about material or spiritual needs. In this way, it has neutralized the difference between subjects in favor of more abstract and, whenever possible, universal codes. But this economy needs to be rethought because it brings a loss of subjectivity and a loss of meaning.

We need to start again from the relationships between words, gesture and meaning in an incarnate subject — a subject made of body and language — in order to revise the symbolic universe. So, in *To Be Two*, I consider certain sensorial relationships between man and woman. Often I start from the position of the last masculine philosophers who expressed an idea of the subject as body, and even as a sexual body. I show how their position corresponds to a way of being in a relationship that is specific to Western man: a subject enters into a relationship with an object, and not with another subject. As a woman, what I hope for rather is a relationship between two subjects. So, I suggest ways of getting to this point. For example, I explain that the emphasis placed on sensation in our culture often splits man and woman into he who has to procure pleasure and she who has to enjoy it. In order to get away from such a false couple, which is often sadomasochistic, I suggest going back to a culture of perceptions: striving to perceive the other not as an object but as an other, with a body but also with a world and an interiority that are specific to him/her, which I have to respect and desire for what they are. Here I want to mention that in the Far Eastern tradition, there was a preoccupation with an education of perception in one's relationship to nature — hence,

Buddha contemplating the flower and even more so Patangali's *Yogasutras* — and sometimes in one's relationship to the other, which includes the carnal relationship.

F. IANNUCCI: How can we respect the "two" in love?

L. IRIGARAY: *To Be Two* tries to show how to look at and listen to the other without reducing him/her to me or to an object: respecting the other in his/her corporality, gestures, and also thinking about the invisible in the other, his/her interiority. Words concerning the caress lend respect and love of the other as other to the touch. The caress is no longer a gesture that aims to grab hold of the other, in his/her freedom, mystery, "virginity" or "integrity" (as is still the case with Sartre, Merleau-Ponty, Levinas). It becomes a gesture between two subjects, a gesture that gives each one (masculine and feminine) back to him/herself while creating a relationship between the two. In this way, the carnal relationship can become a love relationship in two and not a constant reduction of the one, and particularly the feminine one, to the other's object or prey, unless it reduces the two subjects to nothing, to a zero tension in Freud's words, a "little death."

F. IANNUCCI: Is the invitation for the genders to come to reconcile and form an alliance linked to your feminine identity?

L. IRIGARAY: I made the gesture of inviting man, men, to a new alliance as a woman. In the same way, it's as a woman that I thought the necessity and truth of a philosophy of intersubjectivity based on sexual difference. My feminine identity, which I received from birth and try to construct culturally, facilitates this gesture. Born of a woman, I had a direct relationship with a person whom I experienced as another subject. It's more complicated for the boy, hence the importance of the object for him. Besides, the other gender is carnally familiar to a feminine body: through love and maternity. Once again, it's not the same for the man. So recognizing that the difference between men and women exists is, for a woman, a fact linked to her birth and the becoming of her life, she has to recognize this fact and cultivate it without submitting one gender to the other, neither in love nor maternity.

F. IANNUCCI: Does the meaning of *To Be Two* at once incorporate something quotidian, empirical, as well as a philosophical attitude in relation to transcendence?

L. IRIGARAY: Most certainly. And the title of the book was chosen to suggest this double possibility. *To Be Two* can be understood as the fact that the human being is two, a perspective that hasn't been acknowledged in philosophy until now. In philosophy the subjectivity of the subject is always thought of as one. This "one" is in relation to a world made of objects. The relationships between subjects are assumed to be relationships between fellow creatures connected by nature and culture, fellow creatures who practice exchange at different material and cultural levels. These subjects are always found in hierarchical relationships: natural (for example, in genealogy) or cultural (socio-political, for example). The title *To Be Two* also means to be two in a horizontal, not a hierarchical, relationship. The relationship between men and women is crucial to situate such a social model because it represents the articulation between nature and culture. Rethinking social relations starting with this "two" is a way of wanting them to be more just, less artificial and hierarchical.

F. IANNUCCI: In *To Be Two*, you criticize the Western world as a fabrication by men. What are your suggestions to free ourselves from this?

L. IRIGARAY: Western culture was built from man's mastery over nature, most often through violence. This manufacturing of a technically elaborated world often transforms us into neutralized individuals, interchangeable zombies forced to obey orders coming from the world that surrounds us. Sartre describes this transformation of each of us into "anyone," some "individual" or other, very well. In *To Be Two* I refer to his description of someone going through a subway passage.

The technical universe transforms us into its servants and gradually exiles us from ourselves. We have to find another relationship between the natural universe and the manufactured world in order to get out of this entrapment. Both man's and woman's actions have to be directed towards a respect for the natural world, including the natural world of our body, and also direct creation towards the blossoming of human subjectivity, not its enslavement. So the alliance between man and woman takes on the meaning of a bridge to be built between a given nature — the body and the surrounding universe, to which the woman is often more faithful in her becoming — and the creation of objects, an activity that's more suited to man. The choice, the purpose of the objects and the technique used to manufacture them will have to aim at making man and woman happier and more cultivated: each man, each woman and together.

F. IANNUCCI: In *To Be Two* you talk about the necessity of three silences for a dialectic that's respectful of sexual difference. What does this mean?

L. IRIGARAY: Silence is the place of respect for what's already given: the body, the surrounding universe. Respect of sexual difference itself also demands silence: man's and woman's subjectivity are both inexchangeable, and one can't speak for the other. So each one has to keep an external and an internal space of silence to welcome the other. This silence also has to occupy a place in memory and develop in time. I talked about this in terms of "conceiving" a silence in two, deliberately using the same word that's used for conceiving a child.

F. IANNUCCI: Nature plays a very important role in *To Be Two*. Why?

L. IRIGARAY: As I wrote in the "Prologue," nature is a place of re-birth. Nature is a second mother, but it's also a sexed universe. Nature offers an alternative place for life and sharing in relation to the human world, the manufactured world. Rather than exploit it or forget it, I try to praise it, sing it. Nature also represents a third in the relationship with the other-man. It allows me to respect him and myself; by endlessly going from it to him and from him to it, nature also allows me to construct a history that's more alive, more sensitive and happier.

F. IANNUCCI: What questions would you ask today's feminism?

L. IRIGARAY: First, I have to mention that feminism is not one. Then, not wanting to judge the various feminisms, I'll indicate five points that need to be examined in the present attitude of women who are concerned with emancipation and liberation.

    1. Considering liberation to be equality with man while

at the same time confusing the need for economic status with acquiring a feminine identity, a confusion that's connected to our age's culture which often reduces the human being to a socio-economic being.

2. Forgetting that the alienation of women first takes place in a relationship of difference with man, and that this alienation has to be remedied in that place — a place which also includes love.

3. Thinking that gathering many women together is the same thing as finding woman a valid identity.

4. An insufficient concern for objective ways to promote and save individual subjectivity and collective relations: for example, civil rights and an adequate language.

5. An insufficient questioning of women who led the women's liberation movement and a confusion between historically worthy women and those who opened up a new age for women's emancipation and liberation.

13

THE TEACHING OF DIFFERENCE

PAOLA AZZOLINI: How do you come up with the titles for your books?

LUCE IRIGARAY: I found the title *I Love to You* while teaching a seminar. I was trying to convey that, in order to love the other, one has to leave a space between him, or her, and me, and practice a little in-direction. I gave the example of: "I love to you" instead of: "I love you." After the seminar, the students —both men and women — stayed outside in the street discussing the formula. At the next seminar, they told me that they had experimented with it at home and with friends of both sexes. During the summer vacation, I played at suggesting possible titles for my upcoming book to different people, especially young people, and *I Love to You* was one of them. They almost always chose that title. At first, the French publisher was rather hesitant, but he ended up insisting that I keep this title and nothing else.

For *To Be Two*, I had to decide pretty quickly. I wanted a more sensual title like "The Embrace" [*L'Etreinte*], "Meeting Between Us" [*La Rencontre entre nous*], or "Between Her and Him" [*Entre elle et lui*]. I wasn't sure about my choice, and female Italian friends (the book first appeared in Italy), were against them. I finally chose *To Be Two* because of it philosophically relates to being [*l'être*]. It questions the fact that, in the West, being is always understood as "one" or a "multiple of one" [*étant*]. Aside from this meaning, *To Be Two* can also mean: being made of two [*être à deux*], to be two [*être deux*]. The book's goal is to intertwine philosophy and daily life, and this is perfectly expressed by *Etre Deux* (with a capital D on "deux").

For the title *Je Tu Nous*, I thought about each of us, women, and I wanted to emphasize the fact that it's not possible, or desirable, to think about a we-women without first going through a dialogue between I-woman and you-woman, thus seeking to avoid a multiple that would erase the singularity of each woman and would also run the risk of buying into the masculine model based on the one and the multiple. I also present in this book, the idea that we can't reach a we-women without first freeing the relations between man/men and woman/women from the alienation that weighs on women. I also thought that, our age being dominated by individualism, conflicts and wars, each time someone would say the title of the book — in a bookstore or anywhere — he or she would use the words "I," "you," "we" and everyone present at the time would find themselves assembled together in dialogue and in a micro-society: I, you, and we.

P. AZZOLINI: Isn't your book *To Be Two* a kind of retreat compared to your critique of patriarchal society?

L. IRIGARAY: Not at all. Attempting to redefine, as I do, communal love and life between us, and especially between woman/women and man/men, is quite foreign to the way individuals relate to one another in the patriarchal tradition. In the patriarchal tradition, the subject is conceived as unique, constructed according to a masculine model that guarantees the patriarch's authority: whether human or divine. The patriarchal subject never considers the "in two" [*à deux*] with a feminine subject or even with a subject different from himself. What has changed in my last books is the way I extract myself from patriarchal horizons. After a period of radical criticism, I'm using newer and more feminine methods to bring man, men, to a dialogue that respects the duality that exists between us. I'm trying to lead him, or them, back to the man-being using the path of interiority, the woman-being's path, in order to build a world in better ways than in the past starting from our relationship as two. In order to reach this point, I emphasize the horizontal relationship between the sexes or genders, which runs counter to our tradition, on all levels dominated by a vertical relationship, whether genealogical or hierarchical.

P. AZZOLINI: In your book *To Be Two*, you criticize the way philosophers like Jean-Paul Sartre, Maurice Merleau-Ponty and even Emmanuel Levinas understand the sensual relationship. Can you tell us something about this critique?

L. IRIGARAY: Certain recent philosophers, especially the French ones, have dealt with the sexed body and even the sexual relationship. I object to the fact that, even though they're considered to be philosophers of ethics, they don't describe the sexual relationship as a relationship between two persons, but as a relationship between the man and a woman who is reduced to being the instrument of his pleasure or his journey (Levinas), unless they see in it a master-slave relationship between two somewhat similar partners (Sartre's *Being and Nothingness* and Merleau-Ponty's *Phenomenology of Perception*). Moreover, all these philosophers imagine a complicity between the eyes and the hand, both of them predators of the freedom and integrity of the other.

Personally, I'm trying to save the "two" of people who

love each other through the use of words — for example: I love to you and not: I love you — and also through perceptions: gazing, listening and touching. I describe a way of caressing that respects both the *I* and the *you*, that wakes them up and brings them both to a level of alertness that's often dormant and alienated in daily life. I hope that my proposal to rethink the sexual relationship opens up the possibility of imagining and experiencing the sensual approach in a corporeal and spiritual way, neither a downfall nor an exploitation but rather to a path of two [*à deux*], in as much as we are embodied beings.

P. AZZOLINI: The body and the cosmic universe play a very unusual role in your book *To Be Two*. Why?

L. IRIGARAY: In *To Be Two*, bodies are invited to participate in the becoming of thought, ethics, and History. It's no longer about overcoming the body, more specifically the sexed body, as often happens in our tradition, rather it's about founding spiritual growth on the corporeal, the sensorial, and also on our belonging to a gender. Sensibility and intelligence are intertwined in a cultural becoming that doesn't claim to overcome singularity in the universal but rather save this singularity through a relationship of two, two irreducible to one, to the same, the equal. In order to innovate and maintain such a way of entering into a relationship between us, the cosmic universe represents an indispensable, and also pleasurable, help. It's a place of rebirth, as I wrote in the "Prologue" to *To Be Two*. Aside from the fact that this place allows me to preserve and educate my senses, it's also a third element that allows me to go towards the other and return to me without losing the *I* or the *you*.

P. AZZOLINI: Do you think that philosophy is still useful in this age, especially for us women?

L. IRIGARAY: I consider philosophy not only useful, but as the way of getting out of the present troubling situation that affects the survival of our bodies and human civilization. Also, the worst political reigns are always born out of an absence of thought that leads to a dichotomous and repressive logic. Thought opens up spaces for coexistence, for each person's words, for living in the present and protecting a possible future. Simple pragmatism often ends up in a more or less visible or blind instrumentalization of the other, of the others, to whom a space for reflection and speech is denied: the distance of a "to" necessary for accepting or refusing. For such an undertaking, philosophy shouldn't remain only critique, or merely normative. It requires a certain use of the negative, of the demand, of distancing and perspective, dialogue and intersubjectivity. It can't confine itself to the university context either, but should anticipate a possible readability for everyone, women and men, at least to convey the main ideas of the works.

P. AZZOLINI: What do you think about feminine writing? How would you analyze it?

L. IRIGARAY: I certainly don't "analyze" feminine writing. I just try to write in harmony with my thinking which is that of a woman, at least I would hope to. This implies some qualities or tendencies in the way I write: be careful not sacrificing "beauty" to argumentation and also not accepting that truth can exist separately from poetry; prefering dialogue and communication with the other rather than remaining alone talking to oneself. There are other characteristics: the love for nature, for words which "breathe," for praise and happiness, the will to love in spite of today's greyness. There are so many things one could say, and even more one could read on this subject. Writing can't simply be described or experienced "from the outside": it has to be practiced by writing or reading.

A CIVILIZATION
RESPECTFUL OF LIFE

Concerning *The Forgetting of Air* (*L'Oubli de l'Air*, 1983)

From: "The Air of Those Who Love Each Other" (*Unitá,* July 30, 1996); "Words to Nourish the Breath of Life (*Il Manifesto,* July 13, 1996) and "Words to Nourish the Breath of Life" (*Il Manifesto*, July 13, 1996)]

14

THE AIR OF THOSE WHO LOVE EACH OTHER

BRENA NIORELLI: There seems to be a significant difference between *The Forgetting of Air* and *I Love to You*. In the
latter book, you foreshadow a possible meeting of man and
woman, whereas in *The Forgetting of Air* you emphasize the
asymmetry in their relationship, and the woman's resulting
need to withdraw into herself.

LUCE IRIGARAY: First, I'd like to point out that *The
Forgetting of Air* was published in French in 1981 and *I
Love to You* in 1992, even though the translation of *The
Forgetting of Air* is often published after the translation of *I
Love to You*.

   Then there isn't a contradiction between the two posi-
tions: bringing out the difficulty, the asymmetry, in a relationship to the foreground doesn't mean renouncing building
bridges that would allow it to exist. In *The Forgetting of Air*, I
interpret man's difficulty in relation to his mother and his corporal, natural origin. Instead of facing the problem of a new
type of relationship with the other or the woman, Western man
has built a closed world which doesn't allow communication
with the other, particularly with the other-woman. They communicate only among themselves, the "brothers" who share
the same language, the same subjectivity.

   In *I Love to You*, I say that in order to share love and
words with a man, I have to begin with a: I am not you nor

am I yours, and you are not me nor are you mine. I say that men and women are radically different and that communication between them isn't possible without recognizing these two worlds as different. So, I start from an asymmetry that doesn't allow the relationship to happen if it doesn't acknowledge the negative of an irreducible alterity.

I present this same idea in another way in the last chapter of *The Forgetting of Air* when I say that people who love each other gravitate towards each other because of an attraction that exists beyond all words, all certainty, all being, in the general sense of the word. People who love each other are attracted to each other only through breath, through air.

B. NIORELLI: You elicit many of air's faces: it's an element that surrounds and unifies, but it also carries the voice, the scream that comes from anguish, the call, especially the call to the other, that all too often remains unanswered.

L. IRIGARAY: Air, which we forget too often in Western culture, is related to many things. Among other things, it grants us an autonomous existence. I become autonomous from the moment I begin breathing outside the mother, and this continues to happen every day of my life. If I don't breathe autonomously, then I am not autonomous in relation to the world and to others. Air is what makes me one from the inside through breathing, as well as from the outside. I stand in air, I move in air, it's in some way the place I occupy. Unlike Heidegger, I would say that my first home isn't language but air, the indispensable medium (or vehicle) of communication with the other. If I am autonomous, then speech is clear and allows for real communication with the other, whether it's a man or a woman. But few people are autonomous. So speech remains a cry or a call, signifying a need to go back into the mother. The Eastern way — of a

Buddha for example — shows that one can be born again through breathing; one can receive autonomy a second time, not the autonomy imposed at birth, but rather the autonomy expected from a re-birth. It doesn't seem that Heidegger was familiar with this autonomy of being.

B. NIORELLI: If, as Heidegger says, there's only one language in which we move, how should we interpret this sentence of yours: "Words enter into a new age of their expression: it's neither simple logos, nor is it simple poetry"?

L. IRIGARAY: For years I've been saying that a double subjectivity, a double truth, a double world exist. Doubling, which corresponds to a reality, implies a different way of speaking, a *dialogical* way which takes into consideration both man's way and woman's way of speaking. Such a language doesn't conform to traditional Western logic, with its complement: poetry. It unfolds between two modes of speaking, two languages, man's and woman's. The exchange between these two subjects creates a third language, so to speak, a language that we still don't know, that is yet to be created.

B. NIORELLI: In the preface to *The Forgetting of Air*, you wrote that you wanted to celebrate Heidegger's work while at the same time respecting the differences between you. Why such a close and complex confrontation with this philosopher?

L. IRIGARAY: In almost all my books, I confront Western philosophers. Hegel in *I Love to You* and other texts, Nietzsche in *Marine Lover*, which is dedicated to him as *The Forgetting of Air* is dedicated to Heidegger. I consider these philosophers our era's master thinkers, but their discourse is held within the horizons of one single subject, the male subject. Even though they can't hear my words, I consider it necessary to talk or have a dialogue with them from a place outside the closure in which they stand. I use this approach in order to suggest the reality of another subject, a second subject in relation to the single subjectivity of Western culture.

B. NIORELLI: Could you specify up to what point you follow Heidegger and at what point you leave him to go on your own?

L. IRIGARAY: I leave him at the very beginning because of the monosubjective nature of his discourse. I believe that the subject isn't *one* but *two*, because this corresponds to reality. Western philosophy lacks a philosophy that deals with both reality and life in their relationship with nature, the body proper, and the other, or other subjects. I don't believe, as Heidegger does, that life finds its limit only in death; it first finds it in the relationship with the other. The fact that we are two subjects, that being is in *two* not *one*, implies a limit to the *I* and to the *you* which determines the horizon of a world, or rather of two worlds. Heidegger has a hard time thinking this because he is locked up in a "house of language," as he calls it. It seems to me that he stays in this "house" in order to get away from the maternal origin of his *I*. I can't follow him in this "house of language" for fear of losing my female *I*. It seems to me that the other problems that constitute our disagreement stem from Heidegger's non-recognition of the subject's duality, which he may have foreseen in the second part of his life, as evidenced in his text "the words in the poem."

B. NIORELLI: What prevents the air from being what it could be?

L. IRIGARAY: It seems to me that in our culture — and maybe this explains our lack of consideration for our planet — air has been put in prison, in captivity. Concepts, codified behaviors, and religious dogmas often prevent us from living free in the air, air that can offer us the possibility of being born and reborn every second. Instead, many people go on vacation not to breathe peacefully, in a meditative and contemplative way, but rather to exploit air. The end result is an exploitation of the presence of the other, of others, and also of nature and culture, when what our age really needs to do is return to the elementary and necessary reality of life: breathing.

B. NIORELLI: The tone of *The Forgetting of Air* suggests the peace of someone who has a calm mastery of things. Even so, one finds dramatic passages: moments of abandon, for example, or of death, all the more impressive since you often pass from speculative language to poetic language. How do you explain this mixing in tones?

L. IRIGARAY: Heidegger tried to master the pains of existence in his own philosophical language, but he didn't succeed. Bound to Western logic, showing a great desire to live, he keeps going back and forth, moving from a logic that imposes a certain form of nothingness, to poetry. This poetry — Hölderlin's, Rilke's or Trakl's, for example— is more dramatic than calm because, as is the case with most Western literature, it lacks reciprocity in love, the capacity of getting beyond the dereliction linked to birth, death, and solitude. It lacks the energy of desire shared by two subjects. It's said that, in Western discourse, poetry insures the memory of nature, love, gods, and breath. In the East, there is less of a separation between thought and poetry: thought remains poetry as it was at the beginning of the Western tradition. In

Heidegger's work, it seems that the suffering caused by this separation is visible. Learning from the Japanese master, maybe Heidegger discovered that thought could be poetry. As a woman, I share this point of view. Poetry and philosophy don't have to be separate. When philosophy is no longer poetry, it's often just scholarly commentary rather than thought. Personally, I'm looking for a way to write philosophy that doesn't split abstract logic on the one hand, and poetry on the other.

15

WORDS TO NOURISH THE BREATH OF LIFE

IDA DOMINIJANNI: *The Forgetting of Air in Martin Heidegger* is not a recent book, though it is just being published in Italy. You mentioned that you started writing it "a few days after Martin Heidegger died, in May, 1976. I wanted, I had to pay hommage to the philosopher for the light which he transmitted to me without any obligation, except of course that of thinking."The book came out in France in 1983 (Editions de Minuit), before *An Ethics of Sexual Difference*; *Speech Is Never Neutral*; *Je, Tu, Nous: Towards a Culture of Difference*; *Democracy Starts by Two*, and in the last few years, *I Love to You*, and *To Be Two*. These are also the books that, you emphasized, have greater continuity with *Forgetting*. There exists therefore a bridge between this early text and those that were just written. Leafing through the volume one cannot but notice similar patterns, from the dialogue with Heidegger to the thematic of interpersonal relationships to the mother-child relation.

The Heideggerian component is not casual at all, for in *The Forgetting of Air* you address the originary constitution of the Western Logos and the great philosophers who over time have attempted to deal with the same issue.

And for you, Heidegger is forever part of this genealogical frame of reference, as you continue to try to divide Being into two, man and woman: "To protect the path – you write in your dialogue with Heidegger, while introducing *The Forgetting*—demands that we continue with the

Opening. Meditating on Being I have discovered that its protection requires a splitting into two. Man, by himself, cannot be the guardian of Being, insofar as his vigilance presupposes a certain degree of domination over nature and over language which in the end paralyze the movement of 'letting Being be.' To conceive of Being as two – the Being of man and the Being of woman – shifts and splits the layout of the limit of a world in which to dwell, live and think."

We may in fact ask: why the air? Because, you say, "the element air, whose imperceptible presence is in each and every life, word, or thought, would be the path which allows the return beyond the foundation and closure of metaphysics in order to find again the breath and the spirit which it has captured and imprisoned within its logic." So that whereas Heidegger "hardly ever leaves the ground, whether that of the earth or that of the logos," which is also the terrain of the proper, you give yourself over to the air, which is rather an element of nextness, of propriety, or what allows "not only everyone's becoming, but also the becoming of the relation between each one with every other one, the becoming of the relation between all." And here we have the second layout, that of the relation between man and woman, particularly present in your latest production. This quickly reaches out to the third scheme or layout, that is, to the primary relation every human being has with his/her mother, which as is well known is a cornerstone of your philosophical-political edifice: "Breathing conjugates inseparably Being-there with Being-with. Coming out of the mother, I emerge in the air, I enter the world and the community of the living." Then you add: "With its rhythm breathing helps to renounce the dream of fusional proximity with what gives or gives back life, namely the mother, or nature. Breathing means detaching oneself from her, being reborn, and giving back part of a puff: as air, as praise, as work which is living life and spirit.

Breathing is abandonment of prenatal passivity, that infantile state both dependent and mimetic, in order to ensure and cultivate a status of autonomous living." First element, therefore, is air, necessary both to life and to the relation, which are one. Then why the "forgetting" of the air?

LUCE IRIGARAY: Because our culture is structured according to the removal or suppression of this primary element. Our culture is entirely grounded on logic, where being and thinking coincide and there is no room for a knowledge of life and of the relation. There is neither life nor relation without autonomy, and there is no autonomy without air. It is not by chance that in Eastern culture the wise cultivate breathing until they obtain the so-called "rebirth." Whereas in the West, which does not know a culture of breathing, we have constructed a world that resembles a prison, dialogue is possible solely among likes, never with an other (male or female). To forget the air means forgetting the element that makes individuation and relation possible.

I. DOMINIJANNI: Does the suppression of this vital element have anything to do still with the suppression of the relation to the mother?

L. IRIGARAY: Yes, insofar as distancing from the mother.

I. DOMINIJANNI: Therefore breathing, or the puff as you call it in the book, has to do with language and writing?

L. IRIGARAY: Certainly, I write in order to locate once again my puff. And this breath allows me a writing which in turn breathes.

I. DOMINIJANNI: Many people believe that today the writ-

137

ten text is endangered by the culture of the image or by electronic communication. What is your view on the prospects of the book today?

L. IRIGARAY: In the book there always dwells an absolutely singular relation: the writer and the reader are together both visible and invisible to one another. It is very important to protect this special relation in a culture which turns everything into an image, into what is visible and objectifiable. And into a commodity. That the sense of writing is at risk can be gleaned as soon as you go to a publisher and instead of speaking about "your book" he says "our product." This is a serious problem both for culture and for politics.

I. DOMINIJANNI: For politics?

L. IRIGARAY: Yes, because culture is what guides politics, and must protect it both from an immediacy that cares not for the future, as well as from a dichotomous modality of thought which is always at the origin of fascist or authoritarian regimes. Television politics often does not respect this dimension of interiority and invisibility which is proper of writing, which is the seed of human communication, of a communication among different beings.

I. DOMINIJANNI: At the Salone del Libro of Turin, the Twentieth Century has been defined as the century of women, although the affirmation was tempered with a question mark. Italian feminism, which does not place a question mark after such an affirmation, has been debating over the past several months the end of patriarchy, which means that the revolutions staged by women have overall been positive. However, not everyone agrees, neither on the status of patriarchy nor on the status of women's movements. Given that a few years ago you held that "sexual difference is the question that our epoch must think," what is your view on this?

L. IRIGARAY: I am still convinced that sexual difference is the question that remains unthought in our epoch, but I am not so sure that things are moving in the direction of women's freedom. Of course there have been great transformations in the way of being of women, but we have only traveled a short stretch of the road. There exists still little respect and appreciation among women, and there is a tendency to jump onto the tracks of change cut by some women without fully understanding their significance. And then there is the risk that to the circulation of the "good tale" of difference there corresponds a loss of cogency and radicalism of its project.

I. DOMINIJANNI: Or even a complete misunderstanding: consider for instance the confusion between equality and difference, or the institutional policies that continue to prop up difference as a subset of equality...

L. IRIGARAY: Yes, and we know -- I wrote about it in the Introduction to Je, Tu, Nous -- that at a certain level equality corresponds to the sacrifice of difference, ultimately to its erasure. Through this minefield of sexual difference, I am convinced (though we may disagree) that women's freedom will not continue to exist and gain a hold without judicial action.

As for patriarchy, in a way it is true that it's declining. But declines can still be dangerous. I cannot forget, for instance, the fact that in politics the commodity form is more powerful than representations, or that Stock Markets count more than Parliaments. And economic interests are at the origin of environmental destruction. Therefore, it is true that a certain kind of patriarchy is behind us, but another may yet be unleashed which is no less dangerous than the previous one precisely because it is partly unchecked and less evident in the organization of its power.

I. DOMINIJANNI: Let's return to the relation with the other. As you state in the Introduction, there is continuity between *The Forgetting of Air* and *I Love to You* and *To Be Two*. For quite sometime you have pursued the construction of a new form of relation between man and woman in the register of difference, and you work in this direction even on political/institutional terrain. How would you assess this stage of your work?

L. IRIGARAY: The overall assessment is positive. Last year, as part of a project sponsored by the region Emilia-Romagna on the rapport between citizenry and difference, I visited fifty schools in order to define some pedagogic models inspired by the awareness of sexual difference, in boys and girls, and by the experience of an exchange which was respectful of difference. With Renzo Imbeni I have also worked on a project on European citizenship and he, raised on and shaped by the culture of equality, wrote that in a multicultural society sexual difference should be placed at the foundation of democracy.

I. DOMINIJANNI: And what about the erotic level? What is happening to the relation man-woman in the age of difference?

L. IRIGARAY: The love relation is always the most difficult, even though today we are perhaps more aware of it because the weight of the institutions is diminished and there are more spaces for individual subjectivity to inhabit. The difficulty however is not limited exclusively to heterosexual relations, but to homosexual ones as well. Without knowing how to deal with the problem of relating to others which the culture of difference demands, even the love relation between members of the same sex is bound to fail.

I. DOMINIJANNI: Let's return to the question of relation but this time between cultures. At the Turin Book Fair there have been discussions on the relation between Italian and American feminist theories, and the difficulty of translating between them. Do you have any contacts with American Women's Studies departments or programs? What do you think about the tiresome polemics between "gender" and "sexual difference," and the accusations of "essentialism" that are aimed at the women thinkers of difference?

L. IRIGARAY: My books have always been translated in the United States, but in the last few years the contacts have intensified. However, it has not been easy to overcome the filter which the world of Simone de Beauvoir placed between the Americans and French feminism of difference. As far as the debate over sex and gender, I think we should make every effort to understand one another better reciprocally, to make sure we use the same terms, and to overcome the stereotypes that emerge even among the thought of women. Essentialism offers one such instance, deriving from a theoretical conflict which is contained within that traditional order of philosophical discourse which I have from the beginning worked to deconstruct critically.

Translated from the Italian by Peter Carravetta

LIFE AS A RELATIONSHIP

Concerning most of the books published in Spring 1996

From: "Thinking Life as Relation" (*Man and World,* 29, 1996, pp. 343–360)

16

THINKING LIFE AS RELATION

QUESTION: Your work, like the work of some other contemporary philosophers, puts the universal subject into
question. But unlike many other philosophers, you seem
more able to offer, and more open to the idea of, concrete
alternatives and concrete plans of action for effecting
changes inside the space opened by the resituation of the
universal subject. How is it that you are able to propose positive and concrete alternatives and plans of action?

LUCE IRIGARAY: Do I dare say that perhaps my way of
questioning a universal subject is right and that, as such, it
permits, and even demands both a theoretical and practical
refounding of culture?

So, I do not believe that to question the universal subject starting from the multiple is sufficient, because the multiple can always be equivalent to a multiple or a sub-multi-
ple of *one*. The explicit or implicit measure remains the *one*,
more or less real, imaginary or simply mathematical. The
critique of the universal subject cannot be limited to the substitution of the multiple for the one because it deconstructs
certain values necessary for subjective constitution without
a questioning radical enough to permit the emergence of
other values. Thus, to deconstruct all reference to unity, to
the absolute, to the ideal, to the transcendent, etc., without
bringing about a reorganization of the energy invested in
such values risks disintegrating the subject in favor of the

savage reign of death drives or of the coming to power of an even more totalitarian authority, these two possibilities not being incompatible.

The gesture that I make is different, probably because I start from reality, from a universal reality: sexual difference. The deconstruction of the *one* generally operates either through abstract models or through non-universal empirical realities, in space and time: questioning it is therefore too partial to reach a real universal. Moreover, this deconstruction often is fulfilled in an auto-logical manner, as happens to the construction of the *one*. It is therefore the latter which eventually moves from the real to the imaginary or reduces to a simple numerology.

In order to question the universal subject, it is necessary to approach another logic. The only logic that can guarantee a rational and universal foundation is that which starts from the reality of two genders, masculine and feminine. This logic compels us to rethink, theoretically and practically, the subjective constitution as well as the one of the individual or collective world. The *one* no longer remains here the visible or invisible, conscious or unconscious paradigm, which governs rational organization; this organization takes into consideration the existence of two subjects, irreducible one to the other.

Certainly, this reality of the *two* has always existed. But it was submitted to the imperatives of a logic of the *one,* the *two* being reduced to a pair of opposites not independent one from the other. Moreover, the duality was subordinated to a genealogical order, a hierarchical order, in space and in time, which precluded considering the passage to another mode of thinking, and of living, necessary.

My procedure consists therefore in substituting, for a universal constructed out of only one part of reality, a universal which respects the totality of the real. The universal therefore is no longer *one* nor unique, it is *two*. This forces us to refound our culture, our societies in order to reach a civilization at the same time more real, more just, and more universal.

QUESTION: You have suggested that a critique of patriarchy which is not accompanied by the definition of new values founded on natural reality runs the risk of being nihilistic. What is this natural reality and why is the definition of new values necessarily founded on it?

Epistemologically speaking, how may one gain access to this natural reality?

L. IRIGARAY: This question elaborates on the one which precedes, and allows for the completion of its response. A pertinent critique of patriarchy shows that its system is insufficient account for one part of the real. Without returning to a real more real or more total, the inversion of an order of values is nihilistic in the bad sense of the term.

For me, questioning the patriarchal world has been made possible by the discovery of the fabricated character of my feminine identity. Neither my consciousness nor even my body had free access to the real. I could not move from nature to the spiritual because I was held back by a determination of the one and of the other which was foreign to me. The tangible as well as the intelligible were presented to me and forced upon me according to norms which were not proper to me. Therefore, I had to recover an immediate perception of the real and at the same time elaborate a symbolic universe which corresponded to it.

Let us take an example. If my body, as feminine, was reduced for man, indeed for humanity, to a nature, it can not at all be the nature from which I perceive the world, I perceive myself, and I can be and become subjectively and objectively that which I really am. If my woman's nature was considered as living matter at the service of the other's desire and of reproduction, I could not experience it as a "for me" and assume its becoming spiritual through a dialectic of in-self and for-self. It was therefore necessary to go back to a relation with nature that was not already artificially structured. Moreover, it is in part the estrangement I felt of my immediate tangible experience to these values that led me to question the patriarchal universe.

But I belong to a cultural tradition. My relation to the world, to others, and to myself is shaped by it. I had to, I still have to, effect a gesture that is at least double: deconstruct the basic elements of the culture which alienate me and discover the symbolic norms which can at the same time preserve the singularity of my nature and allow me to elaborate its culture.

This is not a simple thing to do. It requires an aptitude to perceive and to analyze perceptions, about which the tradition of India, especially of yoga, has taught me much. Vigilance in relations to the other has equally taught me to respect the difference between the other and me. Examining dominant values and the wa hey unfold throughout History has led me to relativize the cultural universe in which I was living. And the analysis of the philosophers' discourse has made me realize that the argumentation internal to their system often necessitates bids for power or jumps which bear witness to the partially artificial character of the logic which is at work here. These are only some examples of epistemological interventions meant to question a cultural horizon.

QUESTION: You have indicated that a cosmic or natural order exists which could and should serve as the basis for a terrestrial order — social or political. Why and how should the terrestrial order be based upon the cosmic order?

Furthermore, if men are less linked than women to cosmic rhythms, why should they conform to these rhythms?

L. IRIGARAY: I don't understand what you mean by "serve as the basis." If you mean that it is necessary to start from the micro- and from the macro-cosm to organize a social and political order, then I can recognize in your question a dimension which is important to me. A social and political order which is not founded upon the real is precarious, and even dangerous. All the imaginary disturbances, all the authoritarian deviations, all the cultural regressions are possible here.

I don't think however that starting from the cosmic or natural order is sufficient to build a social or political order. One may risk falling again into the errors of the patriarchal world. In my opinion, a harmonious civil community, an accomplished democracy can only be founded upon relations between citizens. But these relations must be at the same time respectful of the needs and desires of each person and as non-hierarchical as possible, yet they should insure the cohesion of society. In this sense, a relation between a man and a woman both capable of transforming their immediate attraction into civil coexistence seems to me a valid base for a social and political order. Of course, it is necessary to multiply this relation between two as many times as there exists an encounter between two citizens of different genders. But the human community is woven right through such encounters. It is therefore possible to found it on this relational place or bond.

The social order is built on the respect for nature and for its cultural elaboration, only this respect can elevate the relation between the genders to a civil level. That woman lives in greater continuity with the cosmos does not exempt her from elaborating this dimension of herself in order to be capable of a civil relation with man. It is in this sense that I have spoken for her of a necessary proof of negativity in the relation to the other. This being said, it is possible to hope that her proximity to the micro- and to the macro-cosm will make her a better guardian of the safety of nature than man has been up until now. Planet Earth and the world of the living certainly are in need of it.

QUESTION: In *Je, tu, nous,* you write that the relation between biology and culture has not been sufficiently examined. Women should not avoid (re)thinking this relation because it could lead to a new and greater exploitation of women. What are your suggestions about how to (re)think this relation?

L. IRIGARAY: Obviously, I do not agree with the expression used by Freud in reference to the feminine condition, "Anatomy is destiny." The use made of it is at once authoritarian, final and devalorizing for woman.

But what has served to exploit women is a biology interpreted in terms more masculine than feminine. In the chapter "On the maternal order," which precedes the passage to which you allude, a woman biologist objects to the patriarchal argument which claims that the paternal law is necessary in order to break off the mother-infant fusion. In the very womb of the mother, nature has planned a third, the placenta, between the mother and the fetus.

This revelation can only contribute to makw women aware of their liberation from laws imposed upon them from the outside. It invites them, on the other hand, to respect all the more a distance and a difference with the other that nature, in her, already respects. No male biologist, to my knowledge, has expressed in these terms the role of the placenta as regulating third. Why? Would it not be, among other reasons, because it involves the relation between two living beings? And this has little to do with a masculine anatomic science usually derived from cadavers or from animal experimentation.

This same tendency, moreover, can be found in other scientific processes initiated by men. Whether it is a matter of biology, physics, mathematics, linguistics, logic, psychology, etc., generally the closed, the finite, the "dead," the isolated is given preference over the open, the in-finite, the living, the relation. Sometimes one can find at work oppositions between extremes but only belatedly, marginally and not without resistances has science become interested in "the partly-opened," in the "permeability of membranes," in the theory of "fields," in the "dynamic of fluids," in the current programming of discourse, in the "dialogic," etc. Now these objectives have more affinity with the feminine universe.

It cannot be harmful to a woman to discover the reality of her biological economy. What harms her is to be subjected to a science which is not appropriate for her, or to be reduced to a simple nature. To be opposed to a knowledge of nature that wouldn't be used to harm women, this would not be an homage to them. On the other hand, it is useful to incite women to be vigilant about what does or does not correspond to them. It is also important that they not accept being reduced to a pure body, a pure nature, whether it be by inertia or by submission to the other. As I said in "Your Health: What, or Who, Is It?" what allows women to escape various forms of illness, physical and mental, is their own desire, their own will, their own access to the spiritual world, their breath, their "soul."

QUESTION: To what degree does the effort to rethink the relation between biology and culture remain insufficient in so far as it fails to take into consideration other species? That is to say, is maternity limited to the production of children within one species? The relation mother/placenta/child plays a more or less important role in a social imaginary, but are there not similar and perhaps more important relations which are established not only among organisms of the same species but also among different species, as is the case with microorganisms (for example, certain types of bacteria) on which human life depends and who also depend upon humans for survival? Thinking along these lines, could you imagine a motherhood that would be open to men as well as to women?

L. IRIGARAY: I do not have enough knowledge to reply exhaustively to this question. I think I have partially answered it in the preceding and following responses. It seems to me that it has to do with an antecedent, or perhaps a future, of the life animated by consciousness. I would designate approximatively the human child that way: capable of autonomy because capable of consciousness. I am not in a position to elucidate such prospectives, which are partially imaginary.

Shifting the question a little — not so much really — I could say that, to experience maternity, men should encur two cultural revolutions: to uphold life over death, to be capable of a radical respect of the other's alterity. Without these two mutations, I don't believe that men are capable of engendering a life endowed with an independent existence with respect to them. Is it not thus that maternity can be described?

I would also ask: why the will to be a "mother" rather than to assume the identity of a man, of a father in the respect of one's limits? It is thanks to gender difference that another human is engendered. What will result from the blurring of identities? Whom and what does this serve today? To surpass a still unaccomplished human destiny? Why this immoderation? Is it not, once again, a vehicle of death more so than of life?

QUESTION: In your work you often refer to a natural reality said to be living. Could you indicate how and where the line is established between the living and the non-living? Additionally, how is the establishment of this line linked to gender?

L. IRIGARAY: I have much reflected on this question. I think that it is close to the one on the possible engendering of the living by man in himself, on the maternal model. I am not sure that I have finished my meditations on the problem! Today, I would say that the living is that which continues to grow, to become. This growth cannot be reduced, in any way, to a proliferation of the same, to its multiplication nor to its simple repetition as happens in certain physical or mental illnesses. It implies a constant relation between the same and the different, in which is assimilated from the different only that which does not destroy the organism of the same nor that of the other. Willing only the same or only the different destroys life. Frequenting only the same or only the different represents a danger for the metabolism of life. To these considerations, it of course is fitting to add the problems relative to belonging to a species — human, for example — to a kingdom — vegetable, for example.

The existence of gender within the human species is certainly a factor protective of the living because it maintains a necessary economy in the relations between the same and the different. It is interesting to note that the manifestation of gender is assured by particular chromosomes, different in women and in men, whose effect is not exclusively somatic. The safeguarding of life would be in some way dependent on chromosomes not reducible to a purely corporeal genetics. Which can incite us to meditate on our desires for immortality, for eternity, for incorporeal divinities!

153

QUESTION: We will turn now towards linguistics. You are a philosopher who also employs linguistic tools. According to you, what is the relation between philosophy and linguistics? What can each discipline offer to the other?

L. IRIGARAY: No one will deny that philosophy is constructed with language. In the West, this discipline has often been called metaphysics, that is to say a science capable of organizing material or immediately sensible realities with logical instruments which removed them from their first nature. The birth of Western philosophy is accompanied by the constitution of a *logos,* a language obeying rules such as those of self-identity, of non-contradiction, etc., which distinguish it from a simple empirical language. These logical rules have been defined in order to ensnare the totality of the real in the nets of language, and thus to remove it from sensible experience, from the ever in-finite contiguity of daily life.

Philosophy thus represents an artificially constructed language in comparison to what is called natural language. But the latter is itself already constructed and there is an interaction between philosophical discourse and everyday discourse.

The experience of linguistics taught me to reflect on the production of language more than most other philosophers do. This led me to question the linguistic instrument supposed capable of discovering, articulating and transmitting the truth. I realized at least two things which seem decisive to me. First, the language that philosophy uses is not, in itself, neuter: it is marked by a gender, notably grammatical, in a way which does not correspond to reality. Philosophy cannot therefore claim universal truth if it uses such a language without interpreting it; philosophy appears as a partial truth and, in some way, as dogmatic because it imposes as true that which corresponds to the truth of a certain subject blind to its singularities. A single gender marks philosophical discourse in its form, its content, the definition of the subject, the relation to the world, the limits of the horizon.

Now, there exist two subjects, irreducible one to the other. My linguistic training enabled me to verify it scientifically. Man and woman do not speak in the same way, do not structure the relation between matter or nature and mind in a similar manner. The reflection on discourse, on language, to which I was led by an education in linguistics, enabled me to interpret the history of Western philosophy, to interrogate the particularities of its truth and its lacks. One of these is particularly evident: the small number of logical means that the subject has developed for communicating in the present with another subject different from him, in particular with a subject of another gender. Analysis of feminine discourse shows that the woman is much more attentive to this than the man. But she lacks logical rules in order to be able to realize this tendency in the respect of self and of the other. Reflection on language produced by the two genders can aid a reflection on the subjective and objective transformations necessary for a philosophy appropriate to the feminine subject and for intercommunication between the genders.

QUESTION: Your work often seems phenomenological and dialectical at the same time. How do you characterize your method?

L. IRIGARAY: I don't think it is possible to speak of one single method. Criticizing and constructing necessitate different procedures. Moreover, my manner of criticizing is new because it has recourse to interpretation more than to simple judgment. And, in order to interpret, I use several ways, such as discourse analysis, putting into historical perspective, inversion, etc. But, I often use these procedures differently than in the past. Thus, with regard to inversion, as I explained it in *I Love to You*, I "inverse" myself as much if not more than I "inverse" others, the theory of others. To leave the patriarchal horizon required, on my part, a certain turning over of my subjectivity, the access to an autonomous perspective, an autonomous look, beginning from which I was able to perceive from an outside the cultural world which surrounded me.

This radical turning over of an immediate point of view, including on the intellectual level, required nevertheless some dialectical articulations with the past and the future of the History in which I am situated. It also demanded a faithfulness to experience and rigor in its phenomenological elaboration. A certain recourse, or return, to the phenomenological method seems necessary in order to make enter into the universe of the rational some natural, corporeal, sensible realities which until now had been removed from it. It is true for me. In considering the unfolding of the history of philosophy, it seems that it is the same way for other philosophers.

Using phenomenology without dialectic would risk nevertheless a reconstruction of a solipsistic world, including a feminine world unconcerned with the masculine world or which accepts remaining parallel to the latter. The dialectical method, such as I use it, is not at the service of the reassumption (*Aufhebung*) of all singularity into an absolute objectivity to be shared by any subject. My way uses the negative as a path which permits, at each moment, dialogue between subjects in the respect of singularities, in particular of gender. Here, the negative is therefore insurmountable and the absolute can never be unique nor universally shared. The negative maintains real and living the *dialegomai* between subjectivities which, beyond appearing to self and to the other, must speak to one another in order to be and to become self, in order to elaborate a culture resulting from the spiritual fecundity of subjective differences.

QUESTION: In a woman, how can one separate the characteristics resulting from her sociocultural oppression, and the characteristics which reflect, so to speak, her "being?"

L. IRIGARAY: It is important to distinguish characteristics of the oppression already codified in the culture and those that the woman continues to create herself each day. Both suppose a hierarchy between the genders. For example, the linguistic practices which unequally valorize that which is related to the masculine gender and to the feminine gender are a mark of oppression; they can appear at the level of gender properly speaking, of connotations of words or of representations. It is the same for religious values and, more generally, symbolic values which are already instituted. Social inequalities take place in a cultural context which makes them possible thanks to an ideology.

The sociocultural world is not, in itself, non-egalitarian, but a sexist world-vision permits it to be that way. Now such a view is still very much alive, both in cultural stereotypes and in the way in which women perpetuate them each day through their behavior. Everyday experiences demonstrate that women have more respect for the speech of men, that they listen better to them, and more willingly have confidence in them. Already, the mother attends to the will of the little boy more than that of the little girl. Even if her behavior is inspired by desire, it is important to modify it in order to not maintain a devalorizing ideology towards the feminine subject.

In addition to the values and behaviors to be modified, there are others, little known, still to be discovered and cultivated in order to affirm the existence of feminine identity.

Thus, experiences in mixed groups of different cultures, languages, ages, sociocultural membership show that women privilege in their speaking intersubjectivity, the relation to the other gender, the relation between two, men preferring the subject-object relation, the relation to the same gender, and that between the one and a little-differentiated many: the people, the society, the citizens. It doesn't appear desirable to abandon the spontaneous choices of women. They have an obvious value and cannot be considered as inferior to the choices of men. But, it is necessary to cultivate them. So, the preference for the relation with the other gender, proper to the existence and to the being of the woman, must be practiced neither as a subjection nor to the detriment of the dialogue with one's own gender.

QUESTION: In *An Ethics of Sexual Difference,* one finds the description of two sorts of feminine relationships. The one, horizontal, is linked to the relation between women and between sisters. The other, vertical, is linked to the relation between daughter and mother, mother and daughter. What can we do to ensure that a vertical relation does not become hierarchical?

L. IRIGARAY: The verticality of the relation between daughter and mother is linked to nature. It implies a complicity in belonging to the same nature and also the possibility of doing as: begetting in oneself, nurturing... The verticality of the relation to the mother cannot be thought, according to me, like the relation to the father, *a fortiori* to the God as Father. It is inscription in genealogy, in the unfolding of the history of the human species as life. Certainly it is fitting to raise the mother-daughter relation to a cultural dimension. This requires taking up and developing elements of civilization that we find, for instance, in

158

archaic Greece, in Middle- and Far-Eastern traditions. The culture of the filiation with the mother will remain much more tied to nature than that of filiation with the father. Even on the spiritual level, it preserves a relation to macro- or micro-cosmic reality, it remains in continuity with matter.

The rupture with the natural universe intervenes, for woman, more in the horizontal relation. Being capable of human relations with other women, with sisters, demands, from her, being able to overcome her instincts, her submission to nature, her fusion with or adherence to another body. Spiritual conquest, for the feminine gender, goes through what I call "virginity," that is to say the opening of a transcendental space in the relation to self and to the other. This meaning of the word "virgin" is to be distinguished then from the assimilation of virginity to the conservation or non-conservation of a corporeal hymen. It is a question of a becoming spiritual aiming at the maintenance of the integrity of the self and of the other in becoming proper (*le devenir propre*) and in becoming common (*le devenir commun*).

QUESTION: In realizing a critique of the traditional concept of identity, you speak of "relational identity." Could you explain what this relational identity is, and how it differs from the traditional concept of identity?

L. IRIGARAY: According to the traditional logic, identity refers to self-identity, to identity to the same. It designates a reality which is if possible fixed, not subject to change, not modifiable by the event nor by the other. In this way it has something in common with the Platonic idea.

Relational identity goes counter to this solipsistic, neuter, auto-logical ideal. It contests the cleavages sensible/intelligible, concrete/abstract, matter/form, living/dead. It also refuses the opposition between being and becoming, and the fact that the plural of the one would be the multiple before being the two. Relational identity considers the concrete identity which is always identity in relation. As such, it is always metastable, becoming. What I try to think is the articulation between the constant transformation required by a living connection to nature and a return to self which permits a being- and a remaining-self in the process of becoming. I find this place of articulation in the belonging to a gender and in the faithfulness to the fulfillment of this gender. The fact of being a woman, and of having to always realize my own gender more perfectly, provides me with an anchoring in an identity which must not for all that be fixed and unchanged. The specificity of this identity is furthermore linked to a particular relational universe. The girl's relation to she who engendered her is other than that of the boy: the girl is born of one the same as she, she can beget like her mother, which is not the case for the boy.

Woman's corporeal identity is also accompanied by relational characters different than those of man: to make love and to engender inside oneself do not put one into relation with the other in the same way as making love and engendering outside the self.

When I speak of relational identity, I designate that economy of relations to the self, to the world and to the other specific to woman or to man. This identity is structured between natural given and cultural construction. Cultivating one's natural identity would signify becoming more and more able to elaborate a universe of relations both faithful to the self and capable of communication with the other, in particular with the different other, belonging to a gender other than mine.

QUESTION: What is the status of the intersubjective relation proposed in *I Love to You*? Do women establish such a relation more easily than men? Is this a type a relation than you often experience in your own life?

L. IRIGARAY: In *I Love to You,* I try to define the possibility of the intersubjective relationship itself. In the Western tradition, this question is almost absent. But it represents an important dimension in the constitution of the subject. The masculine subject attends less to this than the feminine subject. This probably explains why it was the task of a woman to begin treating philosophically the relation between subjects.

The fact that I approached the problem beginning with the political level is not an accident. It is on this level that masculine philosophers have at times spoken of the relations between individuals. But it was a question then of relations between individuals defined in the sociocultural organization of the world of between-men: the city, the nation, even the religious group. It was never a question — except in an abstract manner? — of the relation between two individuals here and now present one to the other, even, in fact, in the context of marriage. Speaking of the intersubjective relation in connection with a political encounter allowed me to reveal the difference between a feminine conception and a masculine conception of the civil relation. Personally, I consider that the civil relation must be founded upon a real rapport between two concrete individuals. I do not therefore submit the citizens to models, represented by ideas or authorities, but I invite them to a conviviality which permits the construction of a peaceful and harmonious community. Let us say that I start off from the base and not from the summit, as our tradition generally does. It is interesting to note that, furthermore, this brings me to approach as a priority the question of coexistence in the respect of differences, whereas a society elaborated according to an "idea" is elaborated with the hypothesis of equal citizens.

Moreover, I wrote *I Love to You* because of necessities which presented themselves to me: how to engage in politics with a man in respecting our differences, of gender first of all, then of culture, of language, of education, etc. *I Love to You* corresponds to a small treatise of political philosophy that aims toward a democratic organization of civil community. It is amusing to find that while theorists of the same problem claim to found the community on money, on goods, on the army, etc., I start from love between a man and a woman capable of surmounting instinct, or immediate attraction, in order to cement, by their desire, a living civil community. I think that this gesture is indispensable today, including against the death drives which risk disintegrating any society.

QUESTION: Given that the relational identity of a woman is very different than that of a man, how can these differences be negotiated in order to create a satisfying intersubjectivity between women and men? Is it necessary, for example, for men to modify their relational identity?

L. IRIGARAY: Men and women must modify their relational identity. Certainly, women "spontaneously" privilege the relation between subjects and men the relation to objects. The feminine subject constructs itself through a relation to the other, the masculine subject through the manufacture of objects and worlds starting from which it is possible for him to exchange with the other. Let us say that woman must learn to put some objectivity susceptible to being shared between I and you: this relation must not remain, for her, at the level of need and of subjective immediacy, otherwise the *you* risks disappearing as you. The man, on the other hand, needs to rediscover the other as subject beyond his universe of objects. What the one and the other lack in order to realize their relation is a dialectic between subjectivity and objectivity, at the same time proper to each and common.

The dimension of gender can supply the existence of such a dialectic. Belonging to a gender implies determinations at the same time subjective and objective. In respecting them, in and for themselves and between them, the feminine subject and the masculine subject can communicate beyond their belonging to a specific relational identity: the woman renouncing a sensible, affective immediacy, in the relation to the other, and man renouncing a privileging of the object which often leads him to consider the other as object. In such a perspective, there no longer exists a subject in some way neuter and interchangeable. Each subject is indexed to a gender and addresses another subject which is equally so: *Ishe* address *youhe,* for example. This calls for the construction of new types of mediations allowing an inter-communication between the genders which is not reducible to need, nor to instinct, nor to natural fecundity, etc.

QUESTION: How can one encourage people to recognize, in their own lives, the potential for intersubjective relations like the one you describe in *I Love to You*? That is to say, how can one encourage people to rethink their way of understanding identity and relation?

L. IRIGARAY: A first means or way would be perhaps to bring women and men to reflect on the rapport that exists between the extent of their attraction for one another and the extent of their disappointment in the face of the short duration of this attraction. It would be possible then to understand that this widespread reality results from a non-respected difference of identity. This realization can take place, in a mixed group, through the composition of sentences integrating one or more words of relational significance — *with, together, to share, I...you,* etc. — and by the comparison of sentences produced by men and by women. I have already verified, on numerous occasions, how such a simple exercise aids the self-awareness of proper identity and of the difference linked to gender. It is desirable, in the same encounter, to invite, alternately, a woman and a man to speak to a man and a woman proposing to him or her a project to be shared, which takes into consideration the two identities. This learning is not only welcomed but even desired as much by adults as by children. I have practiced this many times, particularly in Italy working on "Education toward citizenship in the respect of difference(s)."

Another way is to point out that a democratic politics is impossible without respect for the identity of each person. It is important therefore to cultivate a real relation between citizens. For lack of doing this, the subjection and oppression of some by others exists, as well as the growth of an abstract energy which serves authoritarian, totalitarian regimes much more than it serves democratic politics.

QUESTION: In your phenomenology of the caress, you speak of the importance of the negative, of mystery and of the invisible between two subjects in relation. Could you comment on these concepts, on their place in your theory, and on the implications which proceed from the inclusion of such notions in a philosophical theory of relational identity?

L. IRIGARAY: The caress seems to me an exemplary gesture at the crossroads of civil exchange and private exchange. It marks the passage of the relation from a link of citizenship to a more carnal, more intimate link: the link between lovers, the one also between parents and children, natural or otherwise. It is about the caress between lovers that I have tried to outline a phenomenology. In part in order to distinguish what

I have said about the caress in the perspective of a philosophy of two sexually different subjects from what philosophers such as Sartre, Merleau-Ponty, Levinas have said about
it. For these philosophers, the caress is not a reciprocal gesture capable of bringing about an awakening to another level
of intersubjectivity; it is a gesture of seduction, of capture, of
appropriation practiced by lovers not identified sexually
(neuter?) one toward the other, or by man toward woman. In
order to go out of this absence of humanity in the carnal rapport, it is necessary to make sexual difference pass from the
level of simple naturalness, of instinct, to that of a sexuated
subjectivity, respectful of the self and the other. This implies
a recognition of the other as the representative of a part of
nature and spirituality irreducible to the part that I represent.
Encountering the other, I must affirm and repeat: you, who
will never be I, nor me, nor mine. Which supposes, on my
part, the consciousness and acceptance that I cannot be the
whole of nature nor of spirit: I will never be you, nor yours.
My subjectivity is constituted in the relation to the other
starting from a not, from a negativity unassumable (without
possible Aufhebung) in an absolute, whatever it may be. No
one absolute can abolish the difference between the man-
subject and the woman-subject. Sexual difference compels
us to a radical refounding of dialectic, of ontology, of theology. The negative, the mystery of the unknowable, are unsur-
passable in the sexuated relation, without abolishing one of
the subjects and blinding oneself by such a gesture. Each represents for the other a beyond of the visible, of the percepti-
ble, by the senses and consciousness, which is a source of
desire and of humanity and which can in no way be reduced.

These dimensions of the negative, of the mystery, of the
invisible are fundamental in the philosophy of subjectivity
that I try to construct. They represent a questioning of the
foundations of what we call intelligible, epistémé, reason,

idea, concept, etc. But they signify one more step in the becoming of human consciousness, liberty, ethics, a stage where ethics is not separated from ontology but remains linked to it as access to the world of another light where the "mystery of the other illuminates" on the path of a new rationality.

QUESTION: In *I Love to You* you write:

"Without doubt, the most appropriate content for the universal is sexual difference. Indeed, this content is both real and universal. Sexual difference is an immediate natural given and it is a real and irreducible component of the universal. The whole of human kind is composed of women and men and of nothing else. The problem of race is, in fact, a secondary problem — except from a geographical point of view? — which means we cannot see the wood for the trees, and the same goes for other cultural diversities — religious, economic and political ones.

Sexual difference probably represents the most universal question we can address. Our era is faced with the task of dealing with this issue, because, across the whole world, there are, there are only, men and women."

In what sense is sexual difference the most appropriate content for the universal? How do you respond to those who see in this privileging of sexual difference a luxury due to a class, racial or cultural privilege? That is to say, even though sexual difference is or seems to be the most appropriate content for the universal from the point of view of a white bourgeois European intellectual woman, is it possible that this privileging of sexual difference is nothing but a privileging of the most classic sort?

L. IRIGARAY: Sexual difference is a given of reality. It belongs universally to all humans. Being interested in it cannot, in any case, result from any privilege, but forgetting its importance can. Because the way in which sexual relations are organized in a society, in a culture, can create privileges. It is therefore decisive, for a democratic management of the community, to define relations between the genders which avoid all hierarchy. This requires a rearticulation of the passages between nature and culture while considering the concrete reality of man and woman and the manner in which this concrete reality can be structured at the symbolic level. Rules of exchange must then be established which allow communication between the worlds specific to each gender, while recognizing an equivalent value in each one of these worlds.

This change of social organization can permit us to approach the problems of multiculturalism and of globalization which appear as a given of History to resolve. In the entire world, there exists only men and women. To succeed in treating democratically this universal reality is a way to accomplish the task that the development of civilizations constrains us to carry out. It is interesting to note, related to this, that certain differences between cultures come from more or less hierarchical treatments of the relations between the genders, at the horizontal or genealogical level. Abolishing the rights and privileges of one gender over another signifies therefore working for the possibility of a world culture. But this can happen only in the respect of differences, in order to avoid this culture being abstract and not real.

Translated by Stephen Pluhacek,
Heidi Bostic and Luce Irigaray

Bibliography for "Thinking Life as Relation"

Question 1: *Speculum of the Other Woman. An Ethics of Sexual Difference. I Love to You: Sketch for a Felicity Within History. To Be Two. Democracy Starts By Two.*

Question 2: *Speculum. I Love to You. Sexes and Geneologies.*

Question 3: *Marine Lover of Friedrich Nietzsche. The Forgetting of Air. Elemental Passions. Thinking the Difference: For a Peaceful Revolution.*

Question 4: *Je, tu, nous: Toward a Culture of Difference. Speaking is Never Neutral.*

Question 5: *This Sex Which Is Not One. I Love to You. To Be Two.*

Question 6: *Sexes and Geneologies. I Love to You.*

Question 7: *Speculum. This Sex Which Is Not One. Sexes and Genders Through Language. Je, tous, nous: Toward a Culture of Difference. Langages* 85 (1987): "Le Sexe Linguistic," Luce Irigaray, ed. *Langages* 111 (1993): "Genres culturels et interculturels," Luce Irigaray, ed.

Question 8: *Speculum. The Ethics of Sexual Difference. I Love to You. Speaking is Never Neutral.*

Question 9: *Speculum. This Sex Which Is Not One. Marine Lover. The Ethics of Sexual Difference. I Love to You. To Be Two.* Plus all additional texts on sexed language.

Question 10: *The Ethics of Sexual Difference. I Love to You. To Be Two.* "La rédemption des femmes," in *The Breath of Women.*

Question 11: See in particular: *I Love to You. To Be Two.* "Hommes et femmes, une identité relationnelle et différente," in *La place des femmes.* Paris: La Découverte, coll. Recherches, 1995.

Question 12: See in particular: *I Love to You. To Be Two. Democracy Starts By Two.*

Question 13: See above-mentioned works, plus "Importance du genre dans la constitution de la subjectivité et de l'intersubjectivité," in *Langages* 111 (1993). "Hommes et femmes, une identité relationnelle et différente" in *La place des femmes.*

Question 14: See texts on the analysis of sexed language: *Sexes and Genders. Langages* 111. *I Love to You.*

Question 15: *The Ethics of Sexual Difference.* "Fécundité de la caresse," "Transcendants l'un à l'autre" and "Les noces entre le verbe et le chair," in *Hommes et femmes, l'insaisissable différence.* Paris: Cerf. Xavier Lacroix, ed., 1993. (slightly modified version printed in *Essere due*), *To Be Two.*

Question 16: *I Love to You. Democracy Starts By Two.*

A SPIRITUALITY
IN THE FEMININE

Concerning *Le Souffle des femmes*, 1996 (*Il respiro delle donne*, 1997) and *Tra oriente e occidente*, 1997 (*Entre Orient et Occident*, 1999; English translation in progress, Columbia University Press.

From: "The Spirit of Women Blows" (*Il quotidiano de lecce*, May 22, 1997); "Breath of the Orient," *Noi Donne*, June 1998).

17

The Spirit of Women Blows

MONICA BUNGARO: Why are you involved with religion(s) in our day and age?

LUCE IRIGARAY: I think that the religious dimension provides a keystone to culture. Failing this precludes our leaving one historical era to enter another. To make such a successful exit, Hegel evokes the necessity of a war. I, on the other hand, suggest interpreting mythologies, beliefs and ideologies in order to achieve a more perfect spiritual realization. As far as women are concerned, I don't think they can achieve liberation through a simple economic emancipation. Emancipation from patriarchal ideology, and also from Marxist ideology comes first. Marxist ideology only grants women the right to be full-fledged men, which doesn't even grant the right to be a woman. Moreover, the religious aspect has had in the past, and in certain traditions still has, a feminine specificity. It's important for women to remember this and reappropriate it for themselves. If God is the keystone of our tradition, I think the most decisive act of sovereignty is to become aware of all the energy, all the representations invested in him. This is also the most difficult act to carry out.

M. BUNGARO: The book on feminine spirituality you put together is called *The Breath of Women.* Why?

L. IRIGARAY: I think that, spiritually, we're in the age of the breath. Centering spirituality on the breath goes back to the most basic element of our natural and spiritual life. The body as well as the soul rely on respiration, the breath. Turning ourselves towards the beginning also seems to be a way of continuing on the chosen path. All spiritual traditions can unite in a culture of breath: the Hebrew culture, Christian culture, Islamic culture, and also the cultures from the Far East. Emphasizing breath is a way of linking the beginning of spiritual life to the most elaborate spirituality, in order to move forward. For women, this choice is especially important because it allows for both a spiritual existence and a spiritual becoming that aren't subjected to patriarchal religious representations. It's really the way to open and also regain a spiritual path that's appropriate for them.

M. BUNGARO: How do feminine divinities differ from masculine ones?

L. IRIGARAY: Feminine divinities are linked to the cosmos, the singularity of a place, daily life, the life of relations, love relations among other things. Feminine spirituality is more mystical than masculine spirituality, which emphasizes dogmas and rites, sometimes in a sort of magical way. Women's traditions are more concerned with weaving the body and words together; hence, they're more respectful of incarnation and personal singularities. Masculine religions primarily serve to create groups or nations of men; these religions are more social, monosexual and homosexual, built in the interest of only one sex and based in this one sex's needs and desires. In History, the feminine divine has shown itself in the form of words and images that circulate in a popular, democratic way so to speak. The masculine divine is more linked to writing and a delegation of power to religious leaders.

M. BUNGARO: In *The Breath of Women*, you aren't afraid to allude to the person of Mary, particularly in your own text. Could you explain why?

L. IRIGARAY: Patriarchal culture generally valorizes Mary as the procreator of the Father-God's son, she erases herself in order to carry out such a duty. Even today, in my neighborhood church, I read: "You are blessed, Mary, for this child." Personally, I primarily think of Mary as a woman figure capable of being faithful to herself. I think of her virginity as the ability to maintain her breath free, to give herself her own soul, and not as the conservation of a physiological hymen. The possibility of returning to oneself, to preserve one's interiority, this would be the way to reach one's own spiritual existence, and also the way to welcome the other into oneself, while respecting him/her. Today such a way of thinking can still help women get out of a patriarchal mythology which has robbed her of her spiritual autonomy and singularity (or specificity).

M. BUNGARO: In more general terms, how would you describe your contribution to the volume *The Breath of Women*?

L. IRIGARAY: Women's movements today are very caught up in questions of spirituality. There are two main tendencies: one is especially critical *vis-à-vis* our religious tradition, and the other is devoted to the study of historical figures of women in the religious domain — mystics, beguines, etc. Even though I think these two practices are very useful, I believe that suggesting positive values contributing to the construction of a feminine identity has become necessary. So, I'm trying to rediscover or invent spiritual relationships between mother and daughter, in order to define a possible meaning for us for the word "virginity"; in order to sketch a useful moral philosophy for our becoming feminine; and, above all, in order to open a spiritual path that wouldn't be based on the separations body/soul, body/words, sex/spirit, etc. As far as mysticism is concerned, I think it has to be thought anew to avoid perpetuating the amalgamation of the divine's advent with the mutilation or negation of life "on earth."

M. BUNGARO: Are you referring here to traditions from the Far-East which are evoked both in *The Breath of Women* and, in a much more elaborated way, in *Between East and West*?

L. IRIGARAY: It's true that these traditions allowed me not to abandon or destroy the divine aspect in me. They also helped me interpret my own tradition, both of the past and maybe of the future. I understood the figure of Mary, and also of Jesus, in a new way. I now consider Jesus as a master of energy that can heal — like Buddha — that can overcome death, and bring happiness. I believe that emphasizing respiration and breath also is a way of bringing in the age of the Spirit, understood not simply as love between the Father and the Son but as a spiritual practice above and beyond representations, which are always somehow idolatrous of the divine. Wouldn't the most spiritual labor be to cultivate our breath, and thus become divine ourselves? Especially if we can cultivate it in us and between us, women and men, or even between followers of different traditions.

M. BUNGARO: And how did you choose the women who participated in *The Breath of Women*?

IRIGARAY: They belong to various traditions, although unfortunately not all of them. There still are other women to invite. I chose women who had already made significant strides in their careers to take part in the book. I know how much it cost them. I wanted to get them all together to make other people, and themselves, see that they are many, that they're not alone, and that while remaining prophets — not an easy task — they have sisters here and there the world. I selected women who want to make advances, for themselves and others, in the liberation and becoming of feminine subjectivity through the recognition of its own specific qualities and its differences in relation to the masculine universe.

18

BREATH OF THE ORIENT

HELENA BELLEI: What does it mean to take care of one's breath in daily life?

LUCE IRIGARAY: Most often we're choking on pollution, stress, athletic performances. We don't think of breathing, even though it's the living human's first autonomous gesture. We become a social body's foetuses, as we were foetuses in the mother's body. But society doesn't give us oxygen like the mother does... Far-East culture teaches us that in order to be in charge of our own life we have to cultivate breathing.

H. BELLEI: How can we, Westerners, get closer to this Far-East culture? Is it only possible through the masters of the Orient? Is the more Western tradition of esechasme lost or is it salvageable?

L. IRIGARAY: I became familiar with a culture of respiration by practicing yoga that disciples of Indian masters taught me. I've met some myself. Thanks to them, I've also learned to sing mantras or fragments of religious texts, which correspond to a practice of breathing that the Western monks often preserved. Reading Eastern masters' texts taught me the significance of their teaching and enabled me to pursue the path without relinquishing the practice. I can only speak of my own experience, avoiding somewhat abstract generalizations.

H. BELLEI: You have spoken of Buddha and Jesus as doctors. Can you elaborate on this observation and explain its relationship to the feminine world?

L. IRIGARAY: Neither Buddha nor Jesus transmit knowledge the way academic masters do. They don't have precodified words to transmit. They are masters who have discovered illuminating truths for the soul, and for the body too, through a certain experience of energy. These people are "awake," as we say. Instead of reveling in their own beatitude in isolation, they dedicated part of it to healing people who sought them because of their physical or mental illness. A woman practices quasi-unconsciously this sharing of one's own life, one's breath, one's felicity, for instance, during pregnancy or maternity.

H. BELLEI: You mentioned women having a reserve of breath far superior to man's. Is this only true during pregnancy?

L. IRIGARAY: Generally man uses his breath on the outside: to make objects, to build his world. Man keeps little breath *in himself*. Women, on the other hand, keep breath in themselves in order to share it with the other, and also so that it will be fertilized by the other, that is to say for the purpose of exchange and rapport with the other. It would be possible to interpret the mystery of the Annunciation in this new way: a sharing of breaths and words that are necessary for the conception of a spiritual, divine son.

H. BELLEI: How is breath shared in the physical relationship? Can woman breathe in harmony with man?

IRIGARAY: It is possible to find a spiritual meaning in the

sexual act. Men, who keep little breath in themselves, come closer to women's more internalized breath more closely linked to the heart, love, listening and words. Instead of remaining a basic energy, physical love rises to the point of sharing a spiritual energy. It no longer is just a discharge, but a recharge of energy. This implies renouncing all solitary pleasure [*jouissance*] in order to proceed jointly on the still unchartered paths of desire.

H. BELLEI: Could one say that breathing is the meeting place for man and woman, and for human beings in general?

L. IRIGARAY: Breathing is both the initial and the final gesture of natural and spiritual life. As such, this gesture is the most basic and the most elaborate that human beings share. In this era of mixed cultures, that is to say ours, breath is what allows us to coexist beyond the diverse traditions to which we belong. It's useful to return to breath in order to rise above the challenge of our time spiritually. The attraction that exists between man and woman on the level of breath is very precious because, in humanity at large, there are only men and women of different ages. This gives us a relational base from which we can build a new humanity, a worldwide humanity, from the most basic to the most elaborate of the body's life and the soul's life.

DIFFERENCE IN CHILDREN'S EDUCATION

Concerning *Who Am I? Who Are You?* (First published in Italian, Biblioteca di Casalmaggiore, March 1999)

From: "Children Divided by Sex" (*Repubblica,* June 7, 1999)

19

CHILDREN DIVIDED BY GENDER

LAURA LILLI: To this day there are many children between the ages of five and seven in Italy, Europe and in the United States who, minor differences aside, idolize their teachers and see them as perfect in all sorts of ways. "And the greatest perfection for them," as you said, "is to have bodily needs under control, something that still eludes the little ones." Then you added: "These expressions of admiration are not the result of chance. They issue from here, within Western culture, which from the first breath teaches to disparage the body, feel ashamed of it, or attempt to dominate it. Or else make believe it doesn't exist. How can we be so sure these naïve childhood fantasies offer clues to such deep cultural problems?

LUCE IRIGARAY: They only appear to be insignificant matters, but in reality they are very meaningful for the child's becoming. Western tradition imposes a disembodied culture and a body reduced to asphyxiating neutrality, soulless. School is the Main Street through which these two forms of death are handed down. And in the name of education bright and vivacious children are turned into adults with physical and psychical handicaps.

L. LILLI: Yet the wars against culture and education have never taken us far: from the burning book piles of the Nazis and the Inquisition, to Ivan Illich's proposal, in the 60s, to abolish school tout court. Only the 1968 battle against "notionism" has yielded some partial results (although it has also produced college students who do not know how to write their own language correctly).

L. IRIGARAY: I would never suggest such a war. We must not abolish culture but rather enrich it while improving teaching methods. Today we are much more aware of blind alleys, and there are changes going on aimed at remedying the issue of educating about the body. We do seem to be concerned with physical or artistic education, even sexual education. But there remain some risks.

The Biblioteca di Casalmaggiore, together with Studio Editoriale Norma, has recently published Luce Irigaray's *Chi sono io? Chi sei tu?* (Who Am I? Who Are You?), a fascinating research conducted among young people between the ages of eight and fourteen, pupils from local schools— selected grades from elementary, middle and high schools— aimed at understanding how children and young teenagers see themselves and others, especially when confronted by one another. Irigaray notes: "identity is more than just biological or social: there is also a "relational" identity, and it is crucial." In the book, it is the young who speak upon being asked to make up sentences with words like "you," "I," "to love," and "to listen." Or to imagine a conversation between a man and woman right after the Creation, when words didn't exist yet. The results are scintillating, touching, here and there somewhat opaque: and they speak volumes about our very young. The conclusion is that the boys say "I" a lot ("too much"), whereas the girls say "you" very well ("too well"). "When it comes to love, for example, a girl would say: "I love you," but a boy would say: "I like you." No need to berate further our crippled and crooked culture.

These excerpts are from the last chapter of a long string of researches which the author (or some of her collaborators) conducted in France, Germany, Greece, and the United States; occasionally these include college students and adults. In Europe her work raised a few eyebrows. "Thank Heavens," adds Irigaray, "as one of the reasons precisely that induced me to begin again with the schools, with much humility, was the realization that members of the European Parliament, when confronted with the expression "gender difference," have absolutely no idea what we are talking about." For the year 2000, exhibits have been organized at the Royal College of the Arts in London, which gathers materials (including drawings) and workshops not only with the students of the prestigious academy (they are between 23-25 years old), but also with established artists (some of whom no longer very young). A similar event is being prepared in Germany. In Italy the book will soon be reissued by a national publisher. Luce Irigaray has also put through the wringer the major cities of Emilia Romagna, a small town around Rome and the University of Messina.

Italy is a privileged workplace for the French star of European feminism. We recall that she was fired from the Sorbonne when, during the "hot years" [1968-77], she published *Speculum of the other woman*, which has since become a classic. There Irigaray focused on that concept of "difference" which sets off European neofeminists from their American counterparts. In the United States reflection has long insisted on an Enlightenment-inspired egalitarianism which ends up flattening the sexes into a false neutrality, but which is in fact male. The results have been noteworthy, but they are also limited to the economic sphere. It is not an accident that black women in the 70s were relatively indifferent to it, and that the new generations (especially black, like bell hooks) accuse the movement of running aground on the issue of securing jobs for white women of the middle class.

On this side of the Atlantic, the theory of "difference" allows one to seek transformations which are not solely quantitative but, especially in human relations, qualitative as well. For quite a while Luce Irigaray has been exploring and developing the theoretical and practical possibility of a culture grounded on two subjects, ranging from grammar to ethics to the rapport with the Godhead. And, of course, with the "other" we encounter every day, for example a classmate. But, she says, "we are not yet wholly two, and the road ahead is still long."

*

L. LILLI: Earlier you spoke of risks…

L. IRIGARAY: In art or physical education courses, abstract technique often prevents boys and girls from locating that integration of their own subjectivity, that well-being which would disclose paths to growth. Models which are too rigid may even augment the chance of paralysis of the senses or of gestures. When it comes to sexual education, teaching in a "neutral" way about the reproductive organs, outside of any affective context, provoke disgust rather than excitement among the youth. In other words: school must end the secular silence about fascination between the sexes, which is rather a crucial energy in human relationships, even in public. As things stand at the present time, the young perceive that the communicative paths toward one another or toward others are cut off, and are often driven to be solitary or even autistic dreamers. To share a life with another person cannot be taught to the detriment of their own lived life, since this would break their individual lives up into two, of which one part is left alone in an uncultivated neutrality, while the other is molded and shaped toward a formalism which ultimately blocks them."

Translated by Peter Carravetta

NOTES

1 Margaret Whitford, *Luce Irigaray: Philosophy in the Feminine*. New York: Routledge, 1991.

2 The Veil Law, adopted in 1975 under President Giscard d'Estaing, made abortion legal in France.

3 The *Centre National de la Recherche Scientifique* is a State-run institution for research in sciences and humanities.

4 "Esprit" is a left-leaning Christian journal published in Paris.

5 The ACGF (Association Générale Catholique Française) is a small Catholic association and publishing house.

6 Today the sample is much more extensive and includes many answers from children.

7 *Se* is a reflexive pronoun that can mean "itself," "himself," "herself," "themselves," "each other": *il se douche* (he is taking a shower), *elle se douche* (she is taking a shower), *ils se parlent* (they are talking to each other), *elles se parlent* (they are talking to each other), etc. It also changes with the different personal pronouns: *je me douche, tu te douches*, etc. (Trans. note)

8 *On* is a third person singular personal pronoun along with *il* (he) and *elle* (she). It can mean both the impersonal "one" and a more personal, inclusive "we". (Trans. note)

9 The orders were given orally and not written in order to retain the ambiguity of the indicated words.

10 *Elles s'aiment* and *Elle sème* are phonologically identical in French. (Trans. note)

11 Masculine plural "they" used for both masculine groups and mixed groups (groups made up of both men and women). (Trans. note)

12 Marguerite Yourcenar, *L'Oeuvre au noir*. Paris: Gallimard, 1968; Marguerite Duras, *L'Amour*. Paris: Gallimard, 1971.

13 Marguerite Yourcenar, *Feux*. Paris: Gallimard, 1974.

14 I often use the word "sex" for the sexed identity. This doesn't designate the sexual per se, in particular genitality, rather the woman being and the man being. The word "gender" is often understood as already codified by language and culture; it thus runs the risk of perpetuating the existing hierarchy between men and women.

15 *They* here is used for *elles*, a feminine pronoun used to indicate a group made up entirely of women. (Trans. note)

16 *They* here is used for *ils*, a masculine pronoun used to indicate a group made up entirely of men, or a group made up of both women and men. If there were a group of 5 women and 1 man, "ils" would be used to designate the group. (Trans. note)

WRITINGS OF LUCE IRIGARAY

Le Langage des déments, The Hague: Mouton, 1973.

Speculum de l'autre femme, Paris: Minuit, 1974. Translation by Gillian C. Gill as *Speculum of the Other Women*. Ithaca: Cornell University Press, 1985.

Ce Sexe qui n'en est pas un. Paris: Minuit, 1975. Translation by Catharine Porter as *This Sex Which Is Not One*. Ithaca: Cornell University Press, 1985.

"Et l'une ne bouge pas sans l'autre," Paris: Minuit, 1979. Translated by Helene V. Wenzel as "And the One Doesn't Stir Without the Other," in *Signs: Journal of Women in Culture and Society,* 7 (1), 1981.

Le Corps-à-corps avec la mère, Ottawa: La Pleine Lune, 1981.

Passions élémentaires. Paris: Minuit, 1982. Translation by Joanne Collier and Judith Still as *Elemental Passions*. New York: Routledge, 1992.

Amante marine de Friedrich Nietzsche. Paris: Minuit, 1983. Translation by Gillian C. Gill as *Marine Lover of Friedrich Nietzsche*. New York: Columbia University Press, 1991.

La Croyance même. Paris: Galilee, 1983.

L'Oubli de l'air: chez Martin Heidegger. Paris: Minuit, 1983. Translated by Mary Beth Mader as *The Forgetting of Air in Martin Heidegger.* Austin: University of Texas Press, 1999.

Ethique de la différence sexuelle. Paris: Minuit, 1984. Translation by Gill and Carolyn Burke as *An Ethics of Sexual Difference*. Ithaca: Cornell University Press, 1993.

Parler n'est jamais neutre. Paris: Minuit, 1985. Translated as *Speech is Never Neutral*. New York: Routledge, 1999.

Divine Women. translated by Stephen Muecke, Sydney: Local Consumption, 1986.

Sexes et parentés. Paris: Minuit, 1987. Translation by Gillian C. Gill as *Sexes and Genealogies.* New York: Columbia University Press, 1993.

"Le Sexe linguistique," in *Langage* 85 (1987).

Le Temps de la différence: pour une révolution pacifique. Paris: Livre de Poche, 1989. Translation by Carin Montin as *Thinking the Difference: For a Peaceful Revolution.* New York: Routledge, 1994.

Sexes et genres à travers les langues. Paris: Grasset, 1990.

Je, tu, nous: pour une culture de la différence. Paris: Grasset, 1990. Translation by Alison Martin as *Je, Tu, Nous: Toward a Culture of Difference.* New York: Routledge, 1992.

The Irigaray Reader. Edited by Margaret Whitford. Cambridge, MA: Blackwell, 1991.

J'aime à toi: esquisse d'une félicité dans l'histoire. Paris: Grasset, 1992. Translated by Alison Martin as *I Love to You: Sketch of a Possible Felicity in History.* New York: Routledge, 1995.

"Fécundité de la caresse," Transcendants l'un à l'autre," and "Les Noces entre le verbe et la chair," in *Hommes et femmes, l'insaisissable difference.* Paris: Cerf. Edited by Xavier Lacroix, 1993.

"Genres culturels et interculturels" and "Importance du genre dans la consitution de la subjectivité et de l'inter-subjectivité" in *Langages* 111, (1993).

La democrazia comincia a due. Turin: Bollati Boringhieri, 1994.

Essere due. Turin: Bollati Boringhieri, 1994.

"Hommes et femmes, une identité relationnelle et dif-fèrente" in *La Place des femmes,* Paris: La Dècouverte, collection Recherches, 1995.

"La rédemption des femmes," in *Le Souffle des femmes* Paris: ACGF, 1996.

Etre deux, Paris: Grasset, 1997.

Entre Orient et Occident: de la singularité à la commu-nauté, Paris: Grasset, 1999.

Printed in the United States
by Baker & Taylor Publisher Services